Bernhard Johannes Schmidt

Narcissism

Asshole Disease
and
Rabies of Western Culture

Fundamentals of Psychonomy 1

Bernhard J. Schmidt

Narcissism
Asshole Disease
and Rabies of Western Culture

© 2025 Bernhard J. Schmidt
Oberwarmensteinach, Germany
All rights reserved.

ISBN: 978-3-7693-8899-2

Publisher:
BoD · Books on Demand GmbH, In de Tarpen 42,
22848 Norderstedt, bod@bod.de
Print:
Libri Plureos GmbH, Friedensallee 273,
22763 Hamburg

Bibliographic information from the German National Library:
The German National Library lists this publication
in the German National Bibliography; detailed bibliographic
data are available on the Internet at http://dnb.dnb.de.

Narcissism

Table of content

PREFACE

Even in a society of abundance, resources are often limited - at least for me. When it came to the necessary decision to concentrate more on the form or more on the content, I decided, as I have done in my previous books, to focus on the content.
The fact that defects in the form are the fundamental basis for narcissistic criticism will be discussed in the chapter on the "triangle of criticism".
And also that if you don't want to perceive the content of a book, you can always find ways to criticize the form - no matter how perfect it may be - and then reject the content because of the faulty form.

When I started working on this book, I was still of the opinion that psychology could be transformed into a scientific discipline despite all its deficits (Schmidt 2020b). And so this book would have become another in the series "Contributions to Clinical Social Psychology".

In the meantime, however, I have buried this hope and will devote my efforts to the development of a scientific psychonomy.

1   Psychonomy

By "psychonomy" I mean the direction that constantly strives to dispel myths and dogmas on a scientific basis, instead of continually creating new ones in any quantity, and in this way ignores reality in its entirety (dogmatically and not fictionally in Vaihinger's sense) instead of examining it.
By psychonomy I mean the search for knowledge that could also be described as "ethological, cultural-historical social psy-

chology". That recognizes and does not deny the continuity of the development of humans and animals, not only in the area of biology, but also of consciousness. That is aware of the mutual influence of biology, culture and social environment on the development of the self and researches this.

And that exchanges the scientifically researched "new unconscious" of social psychology (Hassin et al. 2005) for the myths of Freud.

By uncovering the underlying myths and dogmas as well as the ethnocentric orientation, psychonomy recognizes psychology as part of the meaning framework of a psychonomic species – the WEIRD culture (WEIRD = Western Educated Industrialized Rich Democratic[1]).

1.1   Psychonomic Species

The idea of a solipsistic I, devoid of body, culture and we, which goes back to Catholic dogmas, also largely prevented the perception of "psychonomic species", in contrast to "bionomic species".

It was E.H. Erikson who coined the term "pseudo-species" in 1966 in "Ontogeny of Ritualization in Man" and described their creation.

Ethology (e.g. K. Lorenz, I. Eibl-Eibesfeldt, B. Hassenstein, N. Tinbergen…) contains both the term and explanations of how these pseudo-species come into being.

What seems sensible from a biological point of view, namely to describe this form of species as pseudo-species, is not tenable from a psychonomic point of view.

That is why I differentiate between

– bionomic species that arise through biological processes and are determined on the basis of morphology and nowadays also

---

1   Wagoner; Christensen; Demuth (2021) „Culture as Process"

genetic analyses, as well as

- psychonomic species that are culturally generated and socially passed on through psychological processes, whether conscious and/or unconscious.

Psychonomic species form (and are simultaneously defined by) different, very stable meaning and action frameworks (see, for example, Thurnwald, even if he still assigned the differences to "races" because the concept of "psychonomic species" did not yet exist in his time).

How stable these meaning frameworks are can be seen, among other things, in the longevity of myths and dogmas within psychology. And the resulting blindness can be explained, as in autism (Schmidt, B. 2020c), institutionalized abuse (Schmidt, B. 2022) and in cynology (Schmidt, B. 2020a).

In psychonomy, psychology becomes part of the meaning framework of a psychonomic species, and thus becomes an object of research.

The chapter "II. Cultural-historical" can be seen as a description of the development of a psychonomic species, of WEIRD (Western Educated Industrializes Rich Democratic).

The cultural-historical development of a psychonomic species includes the development of cultural tools such as language, writing and numbers as presented by Lev Vygotsky in the cultural-historical concept (CHC), but includes much more. We will not go into this in more detail here, but will focus instead on the topic of narcissism.

2   Current [2]

When I started working on this book, the war in Ukraine had not yet begun, and so there was no Western attitude towards it, nor were there sanctions against Russia.

---

2   Written in the original German version in 2022.

However, in both cases you can find the characteristics of a narcissistic culture described here:

1. The narcissistic feeling of moral superiority, which is only possible due to

2. the ignoring of reality. This applies both to one's own warlike and anti-democratic actions, especially those of the USA. Afghanistan, Assange, Manning, Snowden, Guantanamo ... are just a few examples.

3. The lack of any sense of wrongdoing (see point 2), and instead

4. the desire to harass and bully others, even if these people have no direct connection with the war, but merely represent a different, supposedly immoral position.

5. The auto-destructive nature of narcissistic actions, because the Western sanctions may *also* affect Russia, but above all they saw off the energy "branch" on which we ourselves sit. And thus create one of the biggest economic crises in decades.

These are the elements that have been a common thread throughout Western culture since 380 AD.

INTRODUCTION

At least theoretically, narcissism can be viewed from three different perspectives, namely the

1. common individual,

2. social-psychological,

and the - largely foreign to us -

3. cultural-historical.

But in order to fully understand narcissism, it is necessary to perceive all three perspectives in their interactions.

The social-psychological perspective has already been discussed in detail in the book "Symbiotic Narcissism as a Group Phenomenon" by Dr. Ganz and me (Schmidt, B.; Ganz, A. 2017).

In this book, therefore, the cultural-historical perspective will first be introduced and then the individual manifestations of narcissism will be viewed from this perspective.

Because it is the past two thousand years of our history that have not only created a central problem in our self-perception, but have also prevented the problem from being solved so far. It is the problem of the frame of meaning that has emerged from this development, of a we-less (Norbert Elias), culture-less and body-less I (Schmidt, B. 2020b), which is not only a problem, but at the same time has so far prevented a solution by means of a cultural-historical perspective.

It is the dogma that the ego develops from within itself, originally breathed into it by divine power.

That the ego, as soul or spirit, is independent of the body, independent of the social environment, and the historical development within a culture that shapes this social environment.

This is clearly illustrated by the concept of kindergarten, in which children grow up like flowers in a garden. Flowers need light and water to thrive, but not other flowers. And the children are given a beautiful environment, learning materials and suggestions for their development - but the importance of social interaction for development is largely overlooked.

Unlike flowers, however, children also need other children and adults. They need interaction with them in order to develop, to grow. Social interaction can only be learned ... through social interaction.

And children also need understandable (see the chapter on resources) group structures, which are increasingly being exchanged for open structures in kindergartens.
Culture is also perceived as a collection of achievements that people have made over the centuries, like money in an account or goods in a warehouse. The fact that culture is an active process that is not only influenced by people but also has an effect on them has been overlooked so far, at least in Western culture.

However, it is the culturally very different developments of writing and numbers, for example, that also influence people's perception, as Lev Vygotsky, one of the most important Russian psychologists, has shown with his cultural-historical concept (see e.g. Vygotsky, L.; Luria, A. 1993). Only in this way is it possible to perceive the culturally determined and also different development of narcissism in different cultural contexts.

Another goal is to use this cultural-historical perspective to shed new light on the individual perspective and thereby resolve supposed contradictions.

The first problem that will be solved are the supposed "Paradoxes of Narcissism" named by Morf and Rhodewalt, for example, here in the area of the individual perspective.

"This may be the ultimate "narcissistic paradox": as they yearn and reach for self-affirmation, they destroy the very relationships on which they are dependent."
(Morf, C.C.; Rhodewalt, F. 2001)

Narcissists are, as will be shown below, the kings in their own empire, which they have created themselves, in which there are no friends, only vassals.
Fellow human beings are always seen as a means, never as an end in themselves[3]. For narcissists, there is no difference between friend and enemy, but only between emotionally and/or economically dependent vassal and enemy.
There is never a relationship in the sense of Morf and Rhodewalt that could be destroyed.

The second problem to be solved is the question of the cultural basis of narcissism, as discussed by Lasch (1980), Wolfe (1976) and Tyler (2007), among others.

---

3   Immanuel Kant: "Act in such a way that you use humanity, both in your own person and in the person of every other person, always at the same time as an end, never merely as a means."

15

The mistake that leads to a profound misunderstanding among these authors is the inadequate, because static, characterization/definition of "culture".

But if one looks at the culturally conditioned development of frames of meaning (Schmidt 2018a) and the increasing degrees of freedom within our culture, then it becomes clear that our culture is not narcissistic, but offers the best conditions for the development of narcissism.

3   Culture and Illness

What is normal? And what is therefore abnormal, sick, deviant?
Does (mental) illness lie solely in the individual, or is illness primarily defined by society, as Benedict believes?

"Benedict argues that the psychological categories of "normal" and "abnormal" are not absolute but are defined by culture. Anthropological research indicates that every kind of behavior that we, from the perspective of our Western European culture, consider abnormal, is considered normal (and even honored) in some other society.
"Normality" means the general way a given culture happens to live out one of the many possible patterns of human behavior; "abnormality" refers to patterns not adopted by a culture. Normality and abnormality, that is to say, are relative rather than absolute." (Abel, D. in Benedict, R. 1934)

So is the narcissism of an individual simply a part and consequence of a (narcissistic) culture, and therefore normal? Or is it an illness, are there pathological aspects within the individual?

If we follow Benedict, then narcissism would be normal within a narcissistic society, and therefore not an illness.

"Most of those organizations of personality that seem to us most incontrovertibly abnormal have been used by different civilizations in the very foundations of their institutional life. Conversely, the most valued traits of our normal individuals have been looked on in differently organized cultures as aberrant. Normality, in short, within a very wide range, is culturally defined." (Benedict, R. 1934)

In principle, Benedict's view is based on the historically developed dualistic approach of "either - or" (Schmidt, B. 2020b). However, mental disorders are in a reciprocal relationship between the individual and society, and are determined by both, albeit to varying degrees depending on the respective disorder. In addition, Benedict's statements lack the cultural-historical development of a society, as described by Lev Vygotsky.
The central statement of the cultural-historical concept is that the original biological development was continued or replaced by a cultural one.
Cultural development leads to detachment/decontextualization from the specific and current situation, primarily through the development of "cultural tools" such as writing and numbers.

„This principle, which I shall label the principle of decontextualization of mediational means, replaced those of Darwinian evolution after the emergence of culture. The decontextualisation of mediational means is the process whereby the meaning of signs become less and less dependent on the unique spatiotemporal context in which they are used. A fixius on the decontextualization of mediational means emerges repeatedly in Vygotsky's account of the sociocultural history of higher mental functions. For him it fulfilled the fundamental requirement of his genetic analysis that different explanatory principles apply to phases of development separated by a qualitative genetic transition." (Wertsch, J. 1985)

In cultures that have neither developed writing nor science, in which the solution to problems has not yet been separated from reality, i.e. decontextualized, myths and behaviors that seem irrational to us are pre-scientific and thus "normal" within these cultures. They serve to confront reality, are attempts to explain and control it.

However, if these behaviors are shown in our literate, scientifically influenced culture, then they serve to deny reality and are to be viewed as psychopathological.

The difference in the assessment of ostensibly similar behaviors lies primarily in the difference in the respective cultural development.

Dörner and Plog (1984) see this in a similar way, but only in relation to the interaction between the individual and society.

"Im Laufe der letzten Jahrzehnte haben wir gelernt, einen anderen Aspekt psychischer Erkrankung zu sehen: daß ein Mensch, der krank, abweichend, irre, verrückt ist, in Beziehung zu Anderen, zu sich selbst, zu seinem Körper, den Anforderungen am Arbeitsplatz, zu seinen Gefühlen verfehlt handelt. Bei der Berücksichtigung der Beziehung ist es nicht mehr möglich, von einzelnen Krankheitsträgern auszugehen und nur diesen wahrzunehmen, vielmehr sind auch die anderen Teile des Geflechtes mit zusehen. Die Bedingungen des Handelns bzw. des gestörten Handelns sind dann zu erspüren und evtl. zu ändern. Eine solche Sichtweise ermöglicht, dem Begriff „krank" eine breitere Bedeutung zu geben: Die Suche nach den kranken Anteilen in einem Menschen wird zur Suche nach den derzeitigen Möglichkeiten und Unmöglichkeiten seiner Beziehungsaufnahme. Eine solche Sichtweise erübrigt auch die leidige Diskussion darüber, wer krank, irre oder verrückt ist, der einzelne Mensch, die Gesellschaft, die Familie." (Dörner, K.; Plog, U. 1984)[4]

However, clinical social psychology also looks at the relationship between individual groups with mentally ill structures and society as a whole (Schmidt, B. 2020c, 2022). It is the degrees of freedom (or "unreality" according to Lasch 1980, "decontextualization" according to Wertsch, J. 1985) of our society in combination with the extensive possibilities of communication, including through social media, that enable the arbitrary formation of diverse groups within society. Even groups that are in opposition to society, such as the "Reichsbürger" and "Querdenker".

In addition to considering the cultural-historical perspective, that of ontogenesis is also necessary, i.e. not only the "current possibilities and impossibilities of establishing relationships", but also the consideration of the relationship structure in childhood. If one leaves the frame of meaning of a we-less I, then

---

4   "Over the last few decades we have learned to see another aspect of mental illness: that a person who is sick, deviant, insane or crazy acts inappropriately in relation to others, to themselves, to their body, to the demands of the workplace and to their feelings. When considering the relationship, it is no longer possible to start from individual carriers of the disease and only perceive them; rather, the other parts of the network must also be observed. The conditions of the action or the disturbed action can then be sensed and possibly changed. Such a view makes it possible to give the term "sick" a broader meaning: the search for the sick parts in a person becomes a search for the current possibilities and impossibilities of their relationship. Such a view also makes the tiresome discussion about who is sick, insane or crazy superfluous: the individual, society, the family." (Dörner, K.; Plog, U. 1984)

the importance of interaction in early childhood for the transmission not only of cultural achievements (Vygotsky), but also of resources (Antonovsky, A. 1997), and the "negotiation of meaning" (Wenger, E. 1998) becomes clear.

4   Culture and Narcissism

The relationship between culture and narcissism is a central question. This question was raised by the title of Christopher Lasch's (1980) book "The Age of Narcissism" and has been discussed repeatedly by various authors since then. Alexander Lowen also said:

"Meine These besagt, daß Narzißmus im Einzelmenschen und in der Kultur einen gewissen Grad von Unwirklichkeit anzeigt. Unwirklichkeit ist nicht einfach nur neurotisch, sie grenzt ans Psychotische. An einem Verhaltensmuster, das das Erringen von Erfolgen über das Bedürfnis stellt, zu lieben und geliebt zu werden, ist etwas Verrücktes. Ein Mensch, der keinen Kontakt zur Realität seines Wesens – zum Körper und seinen Gefühlen hat, ist etwas verrückt. Und eine Kultur, die Luft, Wasser und Erde im Namen eines »höheren« Lebensstandards verschmutzt und verseucht, hat etwas Verrücktes an sich." (Lowen, A. 1992)[5]

"Der Narzissmus des Individuums läuft dem der Kultur parallel. Wir formen unsere Kultur nach unserem Bild und werden

---

5 "My thesis is that narcissism in the individual and in culture indicates a certain degree of unreality. Unreality is not just neurotic, it borders on the psychotic. There is something crazy about a behavior pattern that puts the achievement of success above the need to love and be loved. A person who has no contact with the reality of his being - his body and his feelings - is a little crazy. And there is something crazy about a culture that pollutes and contaminates air, water and earth in the name of a "higher" standard of living." (Lowen, A. 1992)

unsererseits wieder von dieser Kultur geformt. Können wir das eine ohne das andere verstehen? Kann die Psychologie die Soziologie unbeachtet lassen – oder umgekehrt?"
(Lowen, A. 1992)[6]

However, the problem of the relationship between culture and the individual in the area of narcissism cannot be solved by sociology; it requires a clinical social psychology (or clinical psychonomy), which has so far been insufficiently developed, in conjunction with Lev Vygotsky's cultural-historical concept. The latter explains the cultural "unreality" described by Lowen as a result of both the development of cultural tools such as writing and numbers and the associated "decontextualization" as well as the Western European mono-culture of Catholicism.

At the same time, the perspective of clinical social psychology also puts an end to the unjustified equation of any "non-normative" behavior with narcissism.

"Once the diagnosis of narcissism was unleashed in public, narcissism was perceived everywhere; it became a 'perceptual frame' through which a range of 'non-normative' people and behaviours could be pathologized. The proliferation of claims, within newspapers, magazine articles, psychological literature, academic treatises, radio broadcasts, political memos and presidential speeches, that the nation was being undone by the narcissism of others, can be understood as part of a larger reactionary response of those at the ideological centre of American

---

6   "The narcissism of the individual runs parallel to that of culture. We shape our culture in our own image and are in turn shaped by that culture. Can we understand one without the other? Can psychology ignore sociology – or vice versa?" (Lowen, A. 1992)

21

culture at finding their ideals challenged by the identity claims of others." (Tyler, I. 2007)

As Tyler rightly points out, not every deviation from group norms is based on narcissism. And not all groups and their norms are normal in a cultural context. But to understand this, a critical analysis of the theoretical premises and postulates of psychology is required.

"But on principle it is quite wrong to try founding a theory on observable magnitudes alone. In reality the very opposite happens. It is the theory which decides what we can observe." So wrote Einstein to Werner Heisenberg, a year before Heisenberg formulated his indeterminacy principle in 1927. "It is the theory which decides what we can observe"—that is the exact reverse of the test-theory-by-facts methodology by which the philosophers say science always proceeds."
(Broad; Wade 1982)

It is above all the postulate of the we-, body- and culture-less I (Schmidt, B. 2020b), and thus the previous lack of a clinical social psychology, that needs to be questioned.

"Jede Wissenschaft, welche nicht beschreiben, sondern erklären (also kausal verfahren) will, muß anheben mit dem Untersuchen der Prinzipien ihres Erklärens. Andernfalls geschieht ihr mit Sicherheit, daß sie als Erfahrungstatsache behandelt, was in Wahrheit vermöge des Erklärungsprinzips erst gesetzt wird. Nehme ich z. B. ganz weite Erklärungsgründe, wie z. B. „Wille zur Macht", „Selbsterhaltung", „Libido" (Lustverlangen), also Unvermeidlichkeiten, welche in Alles und Jedes sicher mit eingehn, und beginne nun auf Grund eines so allgemeinen Erklärungsprinzipes Erscheinungen des Seelenlebens wie das Träumen, Glauben, Sehnsüchtigsein, Lieben, Schwärmen usw. zu analysieren, so versteht es sich von selbst, daß ich um eine schon vorgegebene Invariante die Wahrnehmungen aufreihe und anordne." (Lessing, Th. 1929/2021)[7]

5   Narcissistic culture?

A. Lowen (1992) is right in pointing out the connection between culture and the individual, i.e. the interdependence of development.

"Claims that consumer-orientated and media-saturated cultures have given rise to 'a new narcissism' have been repeatedly asserted within social and cultural criticism for the past 40 years. Within cultural studies there has been a recent proliferation of accounts of the rise of narcissism in analyses of consumer culture, celebrity culture and new media. Returning to key influential accounts of 'cultural narcissism' that emerged in social criticism and popular media in the 1970s, this article interrogates the claim that narcissism is the pathology of our time." (Tyler, I. 2007)

Pathology of our time? Yes!
How and why will be explained below.

---

7   "Every science that does not want to describe but to explain (i.e. to proceed causally) must begin by examining the principles of its explanation. Otherwise it will certainly treat as an empirical fact what is in truth only posited by means of the principle of explanation.
If, for example, I take very broad explanatory grounds, such as "will to power", "self-preservation", "libido" (desire for pleasure), i.e. inevitabilities that are certainly included in everything and everyone, and then begin to analyze phenomena of the mental life such as dreaming, believing, longing, loving, infatuation, etc. on the basis of such a general explanatory principle, then it goes without saying that I line up and arrange the perceptions around an already given invariant." (Lessing, Th. 1929/2021)

But can a culture be "sick", can it be or become narcissistic? No!

But it can do three things.
Firstly, culture can offer the degrees of freedom that are helpful or necessary for the development of mental disorders. The need to adapt to the physical and social environment can be reduced by a technologically affluent society. Only the development of an affluent society based on technological progress makes "un-reality" possible. Just one or two centuries ago, this was only reserved for a very small group due to the daily challenges.

Furthermore, a culture can create conditions that encourage the development of narcissistic disorders, as will be shown in the section on pathogenesis.

And in addition, a framework of meaning can arise within a culture due to cultural-historical development that makes the perception of a mental disorder difficult or even impossible. It is the historically developed definition, or rather the dogma, that the I is we-, culture- and body-less (Schmidt, B. 2020b).

It is the developments of the last 1,600 years or so that have shaped our understanding of people and the environment, our philosophy and psychology.
To recognize this, one must detach oneself as much as possible from one's own culturally conditioned perception and view one's own cultural development as neutrally as possible.
Because through our own historical development, the irrational becomes so familiar to us, so much so that it becomes a frame-work of meaning, that it appears rational to us and we define it as rational.

We are trapped in this "frame of meaning" that is socially transmitted to us from an early age.

6   Asshole?

"Asshole" is a harsh word, but it gets to the heart of the relationship between the narcissistic personality and its environment. It is the identification of the symptom complex that accompanies the narcissistic personality disorder that can justify this term.

The symptoms that will be described in more detail later on - including their necessary connection - do not always occur in the same form, of course. But they are all necessarily present because they are mutually dependent.

The symptom complex consists of the following components:

- Megalomania
- Refusal to perceive reality
- Mythomania
- Dogmatic, ideological, intolerant, missionary
- Manipulative
- Lack of empathy or existing pseudo-empathy, such as in animal rights activists (Schmidt, B. 2022)
- Lack of awareness of injustice (Schmidt, B. 2022)
- Extremely hurtful, destructive

Once the symptom complex has been identified as such, it will be found in Emperor Theodosius, the Inquisition, dictators, terrorist regimes, the RAF, and up to our time in cancel culture[8].

---

8   See e.g. Scherrer, L. (2021): Politisches Mobbing an der Universität: der Fall Klaus Kinzler

The perception and definition of mental illness is therefore not only socially conditioned, but also culturally and historically. And this in two directions.

On the one hand, it is the respective cultural level of development that defines mythological-irrational behavior as psychopathy.

And on the other hand, how psychopathy manifests itself at the respective cultural level, depending on the degrees of freedom ("unreality") offered.

7   Disease

There are several problems in connection with the perception of narcissism as an illness.

Firstly, this classification is extremely difficult given the symptom complex at hand.

Anyone who has fallen into the "trap" of a narcissist, into the targeted economic and/or emotional dependency, and has been subjected to compulsive bullying and harassment by them, will find it difficult to perceive them as suffering/sick people.

Secondly, a corresponding framework of meaning is required, which, however, as already mentioned and will be shown in more detail below, stands in the way of precisely this recognition in our culture.

And thirdly, the narcissistic personality disorder primarily causes a profound developmental disorder, which sometimes only leads to problems late in life, e.g. decompensation.

7.1   There is NO "Primary Narcissism"

The idea of primary narcissism, as found in Freud and Piaget, among others, comes from the idea of a solipsistic ego that develops from within, i.e. without the need for social interaction. It is the idea of the development of an ego that develops from the inside out.

In contrast, and with good reason, Lev Vygotsky takes the opposite position. According to Vygotsky, from the first breath onwards, humans are socially interacting beings that develop from the outside in.

The question in relation to illness, therefore, according to Vygotsky, must not only be what illness a person has, and not just which person has the illness, but:

Which person in which culture has which illness?

7.2   And also NO "Positive Narcissism"

Just as there is no such thing as positive rheumatism or positive hemorrhoids, there is also no such thing as positive narcissism. An asshole is and remains an asshole.

"In short, we suggest that both the layperson's and the psychologist's fascination with narcissism lies in the challenges inherent in understanding the underlying psychological dynamics of narcissistic behavior." (Morf; Rhodewalt 2001)

Anyone who is fascinated by narcissists has never really met one! Anyone who is fascinated by narcissists only knows the manipulative facade, the flashing bait that is supposed to lure you in and lead you into dependency.

Anyone who has fallen into the clutches of a narcissist, into actively induced dependency, loses all fascination[9].

The "Paradoxes of Narcissism" (Morf; Rhodewalt 2001) disappear when one questions one's own culturally developed and transmitted thought principles, as will be done below. Because then the basic mechanisms and almost inevitable consequences become visible.

8   Rabies

The comparison of narcissism with rabies is justified by three characteristics.

Firstly, rabies has a very long incubation period, i.e. the time between infection and the appearance of symptoms. This long incubation period, which can also be years, makes the diagnosis of rabies difficult.

Secondly, the behavior of infected animals changes in such a way that they actively contribute to the spread of the rabies virus. Both through the loss of natural shyness and through the behavior that is described by the German name "Tollwut".

Rabid animals are therefore infectious in two ways: as carriers of the virus and through their changed behavior.

And thirdly, once clinical symptoms appear, rabies is no longer curable.

In narcissism, too, as will be explained later, the incubation period between infection, which can be dated almost exactly to the year 380 AD, and the development of symptoms is very long.

Due to the lack of a cultural-HISTORICAL perspective, Wolfe, Lasch and Tyler confuse the massive occurrence of clinical

---

9   See e.g. Schmidt, B. (2018b)

symptoms in our time with both the disease itself and the infection that causes it.

The questions to be answered are:
1. the type of infection
2. the course of symptom development
3. infectiousness

The narcissism of Western culture was infectious from the very beginning. And this was primarily due to the changed behavior.

Western man became a "culturally disguised predatory ape" (Theodor Lessing), who mercilessly defended the grace of God that he had bestowed on himself and forced it on others. And not without robbing the affected countries, destroying their cultures and killing their indigenous populations...

The incubation period lasted for many centuries until the development of symptoms on the current, culture-pervading scale became possible.

And it can be assumed that Western culture, like many other cultures before it, will perish from narcissism. The supposedly impending downfall of the Western world or the earth has of course already been discussed by other authors, for example by
- Theodor Lessing in "Europe and Asia. The downfall of the earth due to the spirit"
- Oswald Spranger in "The downfall of the West"
The causes and circumstances that will lead to the downfall will not be discussed in detail or directly here. These will emerge indirectly from the further explanations.

CULTURAL-HISTORICAL

The first part will examine the cultural-historical development,
i.e. the course of the disease of narcissism as the "rabies" of
Western culture, from infection through the incubation period
to the current manifestation of clinical symptoms.
Similar developments have occurred before and will continue
to occur in the future. Reference is made here to Lewis Mumford's book (1986) "The Myth of the Machine". In this, Mumford describes both the developments in other cultures and parallels to our current culture.

9   Infection

Because of our cultural background, we generally equate religiosity with Catholicism. But this is not a necessary, and in fact a
false, equation, because

• Religiosity is not the same as monotheism.

• Monotheism is not the same as Christianity.

Christianity is not the same as Catholicism.

The development of this false equation was presented quite generally in the "Entwurf einer wissenschaftlichen Psychologie"
(Schmidt, B. 2020b), and at the same time the basic postulates
and premises of previous psychology were questioned.
Here, this development of religious ideas will be discussed in
more detail, because it is necessary for understanding narcissism.

It is a twofold step that took place around 2,000 years ago and still shapes our self-image and perception today.

It is the step from Judaism to Christianity, and then from Christianity to Catholicism of Western European origin.

9.1 Judaism

You are a Jew from birth. And as a Jew you are part of the chosen people, and therefore a member of a special covenant with God.

"Im Gegensatz zu jeder andern Religion jedoch ist die mosaische untrennbar mit der Idee eines besonderen Volkes verknüpft. Man kann Katholik oder Protestant, Mohammedaner oder Buddhist sein, unabhängig von Volk oder Rasse. Der jüdische Glaube dagegen setzt die Zugehörigkeit zu einem historischen Volk voraus, mit einem eigenen Land, aus dem es zeitweilig vertrieben wurde." (Koestler, A. 1980)[10]

The Jewish faith is therefore tied to a people and its homeland, and represents a collective connection of this people with God.

"Christentum und Islam verlangen von ihren Anhängern nur, daß sie gewisse Lehren und ethische Vorschriften akzeptieren, die über Grenzen und Völker hinausgehen; der gläubige Jude bezeichnet sich als Angehörigen des Auserwählten Volkes, als Nachkomme Abrahams, Isaaks und Jakobs, mit denen Gott einen Bund eingegangen ist, der das Versprechen bevorzugter

---

10   "Unlike any other religion, however, the Mosaic religion is inseparably linked to the idea of a particular people. One can be Catholic or Protestant, Mohammedan or Buddhist, regardless of people or race. The Jewish faith, on the other hand, presupposes belonging to a historical people, with its own country from which it was temporarily expelled." (Koestler, A. 1980)

Behandlung und einer geographischen Heimat einschließt."
(Koestler, A. 1980)[11]

This belonging to the chosen people from birth has several consequences.

Firstly, the belief is a collective one, concerning the people as a whole.

Secondly, the belief is based on a traditional myth and does not need to be backed up by dogma.

As a result, missionizing is of course not possible in any way.

9.1.a   Collective

Judaism is based on the belief in a connection with God as a people, not as an individual.

It is the covenant between God and the people of Israel.

The whole relationship with God is therefore of a collective nature.

"Im fünfbändigen Jüdischen Lexikon (Jüdischer Verlag Berlin) findet der Leser weitere Belege für die Kollektivschuld der jüdischen Gesamtheitsseele unter den Stichworten »Arewut« (Solidarhaftung); Kilal Jisroel (Allheit des Volkes) und Widduj (Schuldbekenntnis).

Einige wichtige Stellen seien hier angeführt:

»Das Bekenntnis zu allen erdenklichen moralischen Verfehlungen, die in Wirklichkeit sich kaum bei einem einzigen Menschen vereinigt finden dürften, entsprang dem Kollektivcharak-

---

11   "Christianity and Islam only require their followers to accept certain teachings and ethical rules that transcend borders and peoples; the believing Jew describes himself as a member of the chosen people, as a descendant of Abraham, Isaac and Jacob, with whom God has entered into a covenant that includes the promise of preferential treatment and a geographical homeland." (Koestler, A. 1980)

ter des jüdischen Gottesdienstes und Gebets; hier betet weniger der einzelne Jude als vielmehr die jüdische Gesamtseele. Zugleich wurde es als wohltuend empfunden, daß, indem alle sich zu allen Sünden bekannten, dem Einzelnen die Beschämung erspart blieb, seine tatsächliche besondere Sünde zu nennen.«" (Lessing, Th. 1930)[12]

9.1.b   Not dogmatic

The rabbis are scribes who study the traditional scriptures, interpret them and communicate them to believers. They are not, as in Catholicism with its hierarchical structure from the Pope down to the priests, supposed representatives of God on earth. There is therefore no claim to power that would have to be supported by dogma.

9.1.c   Not missionary

One is a Jew, and thus part of the chosen people, by birth, which is why missionizing would of course make no sense. But the dualistic separation between God and the devil[13] is also

---

12   "In the five-volume Jewish Encyclopedia (Jewish Publishers Berlin), the reader will find further evidence of the collective guilt of the Jewish soul as a whole under the keywords "Arewut" (solidarity); Kilal Yisroel (all of the people) and Widduj (confession of guilt). Some important passages are cited here:

"The confession of all imaginable moral transgressions, which in reality are unlikely to be found in a single person, arose from the collective character of Jewish worship and prayer; here it is not so much the individual Jew who prays but rather the Jewish soul as a whole. At the same time, it was felt to be beneficial that, as everyone confessed to all sins, the individual was spared the shame of naming his actual particular sin."" (Lessing, Th. 1930)

13   See also: Schmidt, Bernhard J. (2020b): Entwurf einer wissenschaftlichen Psychologie

missing from the Jewish faith. So one cannot and does not have to forcibly "convert" "poor souls".

"Indem der Jude ein leidvolles Schicksal sinnvoll zu begründen hatte, stieß er auf die Schwierigkeit, daß nach jüdischer Lehre alles in Gottes Willen liegt und aus Gottes Ratschluß kommt. Das Judentum kannte und kennt keinen »Teufel«, keine diabolische Außengewalt, keine »Kontraposition Gottes«. Sondern: Alles ist Gott. Alles liegt in Gott. Alles kommt aus Gott. Also: Auch das Böse und Schlechte muß in Gott begründet liegen." (Lessing, Th. 1930)[14]

The Jewish faith knows neither dogmas, claims to power, nor missionary zeal, and therefore does not know this dangerous combination of human madness.
But Lessing is mistaken in thinking that it is Christianity that is responsible for the development of modern culture.

"Die Entwicklung zur »modernen Kultur« ist eben von der Geschichte des Christentums nicht zu trennen." (Lessing, Th. 1930)[15]

Christianity is only a necessary intermediate step towards Catholicism, the formation of the "power complex" of church and state (Mumford, L. 1986).

---

14 "In trying to give a meaningful reason for a painful fate, the Jew encountered the difficulty that, according to Jewish teaching, everything is in God's will and comes from God's decree. Judaism knew and knows no "devil," no diabolical external force, no "counterposition of God." Rather: Everything is God. Everything lies in God. Everything comes from God. Therefore: Even evil and badness must be founded in God." (Lessing, Th. 1930)

15 "The development of 'modern culture' cannot be separated from the history of Christianity." (Lessing, Th. 1930)

9.2 Christianity

Christianity represents a massive change in self-image compared to Judaism. The collective relationship to God, tied to a people, becomes an individual one, independent of belonging to a people. In this way, Christianity leads to an individualization of faith.

"Und wenn wir dem uns heute geläufigen Weltbilde trauen dürfen, so wurde am frühesten in der mosaischen Gesetzgebung diese große Beugung der Natur unter den Geist vollendet, bis schließlich eine von nachhinein als Christentum bezeichnete, auch kalendarisch festgelegte Weltwende den Kern des Vorgangs klar und scharf erfaßt mit der wahrhaft gewaltigen Formel: Gott ward Mensch!" (Lessing, Th. 1929/2021)[16]

9.2.a Jesus

About two thousand years ago there lived a man who claimed to be the Son of God and King of the Jews.

"Wissenschaftlich gesehen ist Jesus ein Nobody. Es gibt keinen schriftlichen, archäologischen, numismatischen oder andersartigen Beweis, dass Jesus überhaupt so gelebt hat, wie in den später verfassten Evangelien und Briefen dargestellt. Keine Skulptur, kein Bild, kein archäologisches Zeugnis, kein Grabmal, keinen Satz aus eigenen Hand, keinen Kommentar der

---

16 "And if we can trust the world view familiar to us today, this great bending of nature to the spirit was completed at the earliest in the Mosaic legislation, until finally a world turning point, later called Christianity and also fixed in the calendar, clearly and sharply grasped the core of the process with the truly mighty formula: God became man!" (Lessing, Th. 1929/2021)

Zeitgenossen, kein authentisches Dokument der Juden oder der römischen Besatzungsmacht. Nichts. Jesus, die Apostel und seine Jünger, immerhin an die fünfzig Zeugen, haben kein Wort hinterlassen, das gesichert auf sie rückführbar wäre. Kein Protokoll einer Apostelkonferenz wird uns überliefert, kein Frommer der Qumran-Gemeinde, die zur Zeit Jesu am Rande des Toten Meeres lebt und der Wissenschaft rund 1000 Schriftrollen hinterlässt, weiß etwas, ..." (Bergmeier, R. 2018)[17]

From a psychonomic point of view, it is not surprising that Jesus does not appear in the records of that time, because people with similar delusions lived and live in greater numbers then than today, as psychiatrists and clinical psychologists know, and Festinger et al. (2012) described in detail using a specific case.

Some of these prophets were more successful, others less so, some had more followers, others fewer.

And today they are diagnosed according to DSM or ICD.

The historical question of whether Jesus lived at all and whether he died on the cross like a criminal is therefore ultimately irrelevant - one can and should assume both.

But it is a fallacy to conclude from his life that he was of divine descent, a fallacy that still shapes our psyche and Western psychology today.

---

17 "From a scientific point of view, Jesus is a nobody. There is no written, archaeological, numismatic or other proof that Jesus ever lived as he is portrayed in the gospels and letters written later. No sculpture, no picture, no archaeological evidence, no tombstone, no sentence written by Jesus himself, no commentary by contemporaries, no authentic document from the Jews or the Roman occupying forces. Nothing. Jesus, the apostles and his disciples, no fifty witnesses, left no word that could be traced back to them. No minutes of an apostles' conference have been handed down to us, no pious member of the Qumran community, which lived on the edge of the Dead Sea at the time of Jesus and left around 1000 scrolls to science, knows anything..." (Bergmeier, R. 2018)

The essential difference between Judaism and Christianity based on Jesus is the shift from a collective relationship of a people to God to an individual relationship of each individual person.

The shift from a people connected to God, to individuals created by God with individual souls trapped in human bodies.

9.2.b   From Natural Religion to Self-Deification

It is the shift from the collective belief of being part of the chosen people to an individualistic relationship with (a supposed) God that paves the way for the self-deification portrayed by Theodor Lessing. It is the first step that made narcissistic megalomania possible in Western culture.

"1. Der Hominismus.
Um die Mensch-selbstherrlichkeit des Christentums zu begreifen, ist es keineswegs nötig, an die Stellung der christlichen Jahrhunderte zu Pflanzen und Tierwelt, Steinen, Wolken, außermenschlichen Bereichen zu erinnern, es genügt zu vergleichen Christi bekannte Antwort auf die Frage nach dem höchsten Gebot seiner Lehre: „Liebe Deinen Nächsten wie Dich selbst" mit dem in den Upanischads wie auch in dem tausend Jahre jüngeren Kanon der Buddhisten immer wiederkehrenden Grunddogma Asiens: dem brâhma-âtmanaikya, welches die Inder in aller Kürze zusammenfassen in das Wort „Das bist Du", als den Ausdruck eines Wissens um die „Gleichheit und gleiche Gültigkeit alles Lebens im Unbedingten."
(Lessing, Th. 1929/2021)[18]

---

18   "1. Hominism.
In order to understand the human autocracy of Christianity, it is by no means necessary to recall the attitude of the Christian centuries to plants and animals, stones, clouds, non-human realms; it is enough to compare Christ's well-known answer to the question about the highest com-

A nature myth becomes a dogmatically secured and securing theology.

"Erst der neueren Forschung ist es wieder bewußt geworden, daß wir im Alten Testament den letzten lebendigen Naturmythos besitzen. Aber dieser Mythos ist ja längst verschüttet durch den vieltausendjährigen Scherbenberg der – Theologie!" (Lessing, Th. 1929/2021)[19]

9.2.c   Individualistic

Christianity thus represents the change from the Jewish-collective nature myth to an individualistic self-deification.
Given the choice of being a "nothing in front of the universe" (Blaise Pascal), a "stray of evolution" (Arthur Koestler), or a "mayfly" (Rupert Riedl), or a being created by God, unique, separate from the rest of the world and endowed with reason - who would not choose the latter?

"Goethe und später Novalis gebrauchten für das Christentum die Formel ‚Theoanthropophilie' (Menschvergottungsliebe), worin die kerntreffende Einsicht liegt, daß das christliche Wort „Gott" eben nur die andere Vokabel ist für das Wort „Ich" und daß der Mensch unter dem Vorwande der christlichen ‚humili-

mandment of his teaching: "Love your neighbour as yourself" with the basic dogma of Asia that recurs in the Upanishads as well as in the thousand-year-younger canon of the Buddhists: the brâhma-âtmanaikya, which the Indians summarize in a nutshell in the word "That is you", as the expression of a knowledge of the "equality and equal validity of all life in the unconditional.' (Lessing, Th. 1929/2021)

19   "Only recent research has made us aware again that we have the last living nature myth in the Old Testament. But this myth has long since been buried by the many thousand-year-old shards of – theology!" (Lessing, Th. 1929/2021)

tas' eben nur Sich Selber hebend, fortan seinem Menschentume schmeichelt." (Lessing, Th. 1929/2021)[20]

9.2.d   Missionary

The missionary work by the followers of Jesus began when his prophecies failed due to his death as a criminal on the cross. Festinger et al. (2012) describe in detail the psychological dynamics underlying this urge to proselytize after the failure of the prophecies.

It is then the missionaries who bring Christianity - after the death of Jesus on the cross - to Western Europe, where it combines with the interests of secular rulers and is subsequently transformed into Catholicism with sword and stake. Thus, the former Christianity as Catholicism will become the sole basis of Western self-perception and perception of others for centuries (Bergmeier 2018, Schmidt 2020b), a religious monoculture unique in its kind.[21]

Not only are all other religions and beliefs fought against and destroyed, and the population forced to convert to Catholicism, but at the same time Catholicism is spread throughout the world through missionary work, which was rarely non-violent. The central message is "You shall have no other gods before me."

The missionary work is based on

1. the narcissistic feeling of moral superiority,
2. a lack of awareness of wrongdoing,

---

20   "Goethe and later Novalis used the formula 'theoanthropophilia' (love of human deification) for Christianity, which contains the core insight that the Christian word 'God' is just another word for the word 'I' and that man, under the pretext of Christian 'humilitas', is just elevating himself and henceforth flattering his humanity." (Lessing, Th. 1929/2021)

21   Catholicism is probably the largest structure based on "symbiotic narcissism as a group phenomenon" (Schmidt; Ganz 2017).

3. the compulsive need to bully and harass others, and
4. the denial of reality.

9.2.e   Dogmatic und intolerant

Belonging to Judaism (determined by traditional mythology) and the covenant with God based on it is clear from birth.

The Christian faith (in an individual relationship with God) realized through the institution of the church as an ideology, i.e. as an "exclusive promise of salvation" (Schmidt, B.; Ganz, A. 2017), on the other hand, requires a dogmatic demarcation. In other words, a demarcation of the exclusive, supposedly "only true faith" against all other currents and faiths.

"»Theologie«, sagt Goethe, »ist die eigenbezügliche Selbstvergottung des Menschen«." (Lessing, Th. 1930)[22]

However, the dogmatic demarcation of the church from other faiths requires, in order to be successful in the long term, a connection with state power to form Mumford's (1986) "power complex".
And conversely, secular authorities such as emperors and kings welcome a religion that leads people into emotional dependence as well as economic dependence. An ideology that allows people to declare themselves God's representatives on earth based on dogma, emperors and kings based on God's grace.
An ideology that at least mitigates the problem of coercion described by Turner (2005) by at least justifying the coercion by divine mandate.

---

22   "Theology," says Goethe, "is the self-referential self-deification of man." (Lessing, Th. 1930)

„Coercion is authority in a dark mirror. It is defined here as the attempt to control a target against their will and self-interest through the deployment of human and material resources to constrain and manipulate their behaviour.

...

The more coercion is used the more it must be used, since it undermines influence and authority and leads to attitude change away from the source at the same time as it provokes resistance and reactance to the loss of freedom (Taylor, 2000). The more it is used the more it brings into being a countervailing source of power as the targets develop a collective identity defined by their rejection of coercion and the goal of defeating the coercive agents who threaten their freedom." (Turner 2005)

But whoever rebels against emperors and kings in Catholicism, according to the dogma, is also rebelling against God.

9.3   Cunctos Populos

Emperor Constantine is usually mentioned in connection with the introduction of Christianity as the state religion. But it is not the status of state religion that turned Christianity into Catholicism. It is the intolerance towards all other religions and creeds, as manifested by the *Cunctos Populos* of Emperor Theodosius.

"Theodosius und das heilige Grauen
Theodosius verbietet mit dem Erlass Cunctos populos aus eigener Initiative und ohne Konsultation kirchlicher Stellen alle heidnischen Religionen, widmet den bisher umfassenden konfessionsfreien Begriff katholisch" in eine Konfessionsbezeichnung um und schaltet die vom Katholizismus abweichenden christlichen Varianten mit Zwangsmaßnahmen aus: „Nur dieje-

nigen, die diesem Gesetz folgen, sollen, so gebieten wir, katholische [!] Christen heißen dürfen; die übrigen, die wir für wahrhaft toll und wahnsinnig erklären, haben die Schande ketzerischer Lehre zu tragen." (Bergmeier, R. 2018)[23]

For those who want to use religion to declare themselves "rulers by the grace of God", there can and must only be one religion, one God.

And for those who want to declare themselves "God's representative on earth", the same applies.

The Cunctos Populos is the infection of the Western world with the rabies virus of megalomania and intolerance. It is the beginning of a development that makes a separation of the humanities and natural sciences (with the postulate contained therein that spirit and nature have nothing to do with each other) seem just as natural to us today as the old white men who, dressed in strange garments, claim to be God's representatives on earth and infallible in this role.

A development that has built a dogmatic and at the same time invisible wall between nature and man. That makes the exploitation of other people seem just as natural as the exploitation of nature.

And which, because it is individualistic and antisocial, has so far made it almost impossible for us to perceive abuse within and by institutions and organizations (Schmidt, B. 2022).

---

23 "Theodosius and the holy horror
   Theodosius, with the decree Cunctos populos, bans all pagan religions on his own initiative and without consulting church authorities, converts the previously comprehensive, non-denominational term "Catholic" into a denominational term and eliminates the Christian variants that deviate from Catholicism with coercive measures: "Only those who follow this law should, we command, be allowed to be called Catholic [!] Christians; the rest, whom we declare to be truly mad and insane, must bear the shame of heretical teaching." (Bergmeier, R. 2018)

9.4   Catholicism

If we remember the narcissistic symptom complex, we find these symptoms here in the form of megalomania, dogmatism, intolerance, mythomania, destructiveness... As a result of the Cunctos Populos, a "symbiotic narcissism as a group phenomenon" (Schmidt, B.; Ganz, A. 2017) occurs in Western Europe. A disastrous connection between church and state that has lasted for centuries.

A connection that forces people, not only in Europe, into both material and emotional dependence.

In material dependence, by simply taking away their possessions, and in emotional dependence, by robbing them of their "pagan" gods.

"Ein Jahr nach Cunctos Populos melden sich die Bischöfe zu Wort und segnen den theodosianischen Blitzkrieg gegen andere Konfessionen und Weltanschauungen auf einem Konzil in Konstantinopel ab. Dabei ist die in der Literatur diskutierte Frage, ob und wenn ja wie weit Theodosius auch dieses Konzil inhaltlich beherrscht hat, unerheblich. Denn beide Parteien sind sich einig, beanspruchen für ihre Visionen die alleinige Gültigkeit, geben sich also einer religiösen Ideologie hin, die immer recht hat." (Bergmeier, R. 2018)[24]

---

24   "One year after Cunctos Populos, the bishops speak out and bless the Theodosian blitzkrieg against other denominations and worldviews at a council in Constantinople. The question discussed in the literature as to whether and, if so, to what extent Theodosius also dominated the content of this council is irrelevant. Because both parties agree, claim sole validity for their visions, and thus surrender to a religious ideology that is always right." (Bergmeier, R. 2018)

While Bergmeier's following description is correct, I would deviate from it and describe Catholicism as precisely this connection between church and state. In contrast to Christianity as a religious belief among many others.

"So trägt das Christentum schwer an der katholischen Bürde. Gewicht und Ansehen kann die katholische Kirche, „despotisch, durch staatliche Gewalt und kirchlichen Gewissenszwang geschaffen und nur mit ständiger staatlicher und kirchlicher Gewalt aufrechtzuerhalten", nur mit Staatshilfe bekommen. Ohne das energische Eingreifen der Kaiser, ohne Eliminierung aller Konkurrenten durch den Staat wäre der Katholizismus eine Religion unter vielen geblieben, vermutlich im Status einer Großsekte. Ohne Cunctos populos wäre Mitteleuropa polytheistisch geblieben, Rom vermutlich heidnisch, und im Ostteil des Reiches und Nordafrika hätten sich verschiedene christliche und nicht christliche Konfessionen breitgemacht. Und ob die arianischen Stämme der Germanen in einem polytheistischen Reich jemals katholisch geworden wären, steht in den Sternen." (Bergmeier, R. 2018)[25]

It is dogmatic intolerance, megalomania combined with a lack of empathy or pseudo-empathy that characterizes Catholicism.

---

25 "Christianity thus bears a heavy burden of the Catholic burden. The Catholic Church, "despotic, created by state power and ecclesiastical coercion of conscience and only maintained with constant state and ecclesiastical power", can only gain weight and prestige with state aid. Without the energetic intervention of the emperors, without the elimination of all competitors by the state, Catholicism would have remained one religion among many, probably with the status of a large sect. Without Cunctos populos, Central Europe would have remained polytheistic, Rome probably pagan, and various Christian and non-Christian denominations would have spread in the eastern part of the empire and North Africa. And whether the Arian tribes of the Germanic tribes in a polytheistic empire would ever have become Catholic is anyone's guess." (Bergmeier, R. 2018)

It is the ideology of redemption as an "exclusive promise of salvation" (Schmidt, B.; Ganz, A. 2017) that necessarily and inevitably fights all other religions.

"Nein, schreibt A. S. Bruckstein-Coruth, Professorin für jüdische Philosophie, nein, es gibt keine christlich-jüdische Tradition, sie ist eine Erfindung der europäischen Moderne und ein Lieblingskind der traumatisierten Deutschen. Der Bindestrich in der „jüdisch-christlichen Geschichte" sei vor allem eine Geschichte der Glaubenskriege, der Unterdrückung, des Antisemitismus und der Gewalt. Es sei schlichtweg ein Versuch der Verklärung deutscher Vergangenheit, kommentiert Tahir Chaudhry in der Jüdischen Zeitung." (Bergmeier, R. 2018)[26]

9.4.a   Ideology

A belief in salvation is foreign to many religions and also to early Judaism [27].

Christianity, on the other hand, is an ideology of salvation - as an "exclusive promise of salvation" (Schmidt, B.; Ganz, A. 2017).

The essential difference between myths and ideologies is that myths do not contain exclusive promises of salvation, but ideologies are based precisely on these.

It is the belief in a paradisiacal life in the afterlife, which one

---

26   "No, writes A. S. Bruckstein-Coruth, professor of Jewish philosophy, no, there is no Christian-Jewish tradition, it is an invention of European modernity and a favorite child of traumatized Germans. The hyphen in "Jewish-Christian history" is above all a history of religious wars, oppression, anti-Semitism and violence. It is simply an attempt to transfigure the German past, comments Tahir Chaudhry in the Jewish newspaper." (Bergmeier, R. 2018)

27   For the cultural-historical development of religions from mythical ideas, see e.g. Wundt, Wilhelm (1913) "Elements of Folk Psychology".

attains if one does the right thing.

And what is right, what one should do, is prescribed to one by the church and the state. Anyone who violates these regulations is also violating God's commandments. The classical doctrine of virtue (prudence, justice, courage, moderation[28]) gives way to a good-evil dualism (Schmidt, B. 2020b).

The virtues of Greek origin, which one can realize within one-self and, such as prudence, can only realize within oneself and never in others, are replaced by morality. What one should and should not do is now prescribed dogmatically from outside, and this inevitably results in double standards.

"Quod licet iovi, non licet bovi."

Anyone who acts contrary to the dogmas of church and state is not only condemned to eternal damnation, but also to excommunication, exclusion from the community.

9.4.b   Dogmas

Dogmas serve to defend against reality, they limit the view to a small part and negate the rest.

They make the world their own, albeit very small, kingdom. And so it is not surprising that an essential part of theology is dogmatics, and an essential part of Catholicism is the Congregation for the Doctrine of the Faith. Dogmatically, one defines the world as one likes it, and man as a composite of a soul created by God and an earthly body (Schmidt, B. 2020a).

"Wir lassen euch gern eure Bilder und Götter! Aber ihr sollt uns auch das Unsere lassen. Wir sind verschieden und müssen verschieden bleiben. Nicht wir, ihr allein habt der Welt es verkündet: Gott sei ein Mensch geworden. Wir folgten nie dieser

---

28   See e.g.: Pieper, Josef (1991): : Das Viergespann. Klugheit, Gerechtigkeit, Tapferkeit, Mass.

Botschaft von der Vermenschlichung Gottes. Denn unser Gott lebt jenseits von Form und Name und wahrlich auch jenseits von Mensch und all dem Greuel der menschlichen Weltge-schichte." (Lessing, Th. 1930)[29]

9.4.c A Western phenomenon!

For the sake of completeness, and also to understand further developments, it should be pointed out that Catholicism is first and foremost a Western European phenomenon. And that the madness has not spread equally everywhere.

"Dies alles wiegt schwer. Aber von überragender Bedeutung ist der Verlust der Schriftsprache. Während die beiden großen Rei-che der Antike und des frühen Mittelalters, das Imperium Ro-manum und das arabische Reich zwischen 700 und 1400, ihre Einheit und Kraft auch durch eine gemeinsame, von der Mehr-heit in Wort und Schrift gepflegte Sprache gewinnen, während die rund um das Mittelmeer verstreuten Diaspora-Juden ihr Ju-dentum durch eine von allen genutzte Schriftsprache sichern, verfällt im lateinsprachigen Mitteleuropa die Schriftsprache als konstituierendes Element der Reichsbildung und als Vorausset-zung zur Erschließung eines breiten Reservoirs an Intelligenz und Begabung.
Dagegen ist im Ostreich (Byzanz) das Ansehen weiterhin an die Beherrschung der Schrift geknüpft. Auch nach der Reichs-teilung im Jahre 395 werden Schulen, Universitäten und Bi-bliotheken gefördert, erhalten „etwa 95% der Menschen [...] ei-

---

29 "We are happy to let you have your images and gods! But you should also let us have our own. We are different and must remain different. It was not we, but you alone who announced to the world that God had become a human being. We never followed this message of the humanization of God. For our God lives beyond form and name and truly beyond man and all the horrors of human world history." (Lessing, Th. 1930)

ne Grundausbildung, die aus Lesen und Schreiben bestand"
und können „etwa 10.000 Personen in Verwaltung, Kirche und
Militär gut lesen und schreiben". Grammatik- und Rhetorikpro-
fessoren werden als kaiserliche Gefolgsleute primi ordinis aus-
gezeichnet, das Urkunden- und das Steuerwesen sind zentral
geregelt und die Prozesse im Geschäftsleben an Schriftlichkeit
und Grundkenntnisse des Rechnens gebunden."
(Bergmeier, R. 2018)[30]

Unfortunately, Bergmeier does not seem to be familiar with Lewis Mumford's book "The Myth of the Machine" (1986),
otherwise it would be clear to him that it is the connection of
Western European emperors and kings with the church that led
to Catholicism.

---

30 "All of this weighs heavily. But the loss of the written language is of para-
mount importance. While the two great empires of antiquity and the early
Middle Ages, the Roman Empire and the Arab Empire between 700 and
1400, gained their unity and strength through a common language that
was spoken and written by the majority, while the diaspora Jews scattered
around the Mediterranean secured their Judaism through a written language used by all, in Latin-speaking Central Europe the written language de-
clined as a constitutive element of empire formation and as a prerequisite
for tapping into a broad reservoir of intelligence and talent.
In contrast, in the Eastern Empire (Byzantium), reputation continued to be
tied to mastery of writing Even after the division of the empire in 395,
schools, universities and libraries were supported, "around 95% of the
people [...] received a basic education that consisted of reading and writing" and "around 10,000 people in administration, church and military
could read and write well". Professors of grammar and rhetoric are honored as imperial followers primi ordinis, the document and tax systems are
centrally regulated and the processes in business life are tied to writing
and basic knowledge of arithmetic."
(Bergmeier, R. 2018)

10   Power complex – Mumford

Just as the dynamics described by Festinger et al. (2012) are not unique but rather prototypical, so is the power complex described by Lewis Mumford (1986) as the basis of the megamachine.

"Das Machtmonopol. Zweierlei war notwendig, um die Maschine in Gang zu setzen: eine verläßliche Organisation des Wissens, des natürlichen und des übernatürlichen; und eine hochentwickelte Struktur zur Einteilung, Vermittlung und Durchführung von Befehlen. Das erste war in der Priesterschaft verkörpert, das zweite in der Bürokratie. Beides waren hierarchische Organisationen, an deren Spitze der Hohepriester und der König standen. Ohne ihre vereinten Anstrengungen konnte der Machtkomplex nicht wirksam funktionieren. Diese Voraussetzungen sind noch heute gültig, obgleich die Existenz automatischer Fabriken und computergesteuerter Einheiten sowohl die menschlichen Komponenten als auch die religiöse Ideologie verschleiert, die auch für die Automation lebenswichtig sind." (Mumford, L. 1986)[31]

It is always the connection between priesthood and kingship that is necessary, whether in ancient Egypt or today. Even if today's "priests" and prophets have different names.

---

31   "The monopoly of power. Two things were necessary to make the machine work: a reliable organization of knowledge, both natural and supernatural; and a sophisticated structure for organizing, communicating, and executing orders. The first was embodied in the priesthood, the second in the bureaucracy. Both were hierarchical organizations headed by the high priest and the king. Without their combined efforts, the power complex could not function effectively. These requirements are still valid today, although the existence of automated factories and computer-controlled units obscures both the human components and the religious ideology that are also vital to automation." (Mumford, L. 1986)

"Kein König konnte ohne die Hilfe solches organisierten »höheren Wissens« sicher und wirksam regieren, ebenso wie heute das Pentagon keinen Schritt machen kann, ohne seine spezialisierten Wissenschaftler, Experten, Spieltheoretiker und Computer zu konsultieren – eine neue Hierarchie, angeblich weniger fehlbar als die Eingeweidebeschauer, aber nicht nennenswert, wenn man nach ihren ungeheuren Fehlkalkulationen urteilt." (Mumford, L. 1986)[32]

The connection between the predatory warriors and the priests leads to what Lessing calls the "culturally disguised predatory ape."

"Die Wirksamkeit des Königtums beruht in der gesamten Geschichte auf eben dieser Verbindung der räuberischen Tapferkeit und Führerschaft des Jägers mit der Sternkunde und göttlichen Eingebung des Priesters. In primitiveren Gesellschaften wurden diese Aufgaben lange Zeit von einem Kriegshäuptling und einem Friedenshäuptling getrennt repräsentiert. In beiden Fällen beruhten die magischen Attribute des Königtums auf besonderer funktioneller Eignung – der Bereitschaft, Verantwortung zu tragen und Führungsentscheidungen zu treffen. Die Führung wurde von der Priesterschaft unterstützt, die die Naturerscheinungen beobachtete und die Fähigkeit besaß, Zeichen zu deuten, Wissen zu sammeln und die Ausführung von Befehlen zu sichern.

Der König beanspruchte und erhielt die Macht über Leben und Tod der ganzen Gemeinschaft. Diese Art und Weise, in einem

---

32 "No king could rule safely and effectively without the aid of such organized 'higher knowledge,' just as today the Pentagon cannot take a step without consulting its specialized scientists, experts, game theorists, and computers—a new hierarchy, supposedly less fallible than the viscera inspectors, but not worth mentioning, judging by its egregious miscalculations." (Mumford, L. 1986)

großen Gebiet Kooperation herzustellen, steht im Gegensatz zu den bescheidenen Lebensformen des Bauerndorfes, dessen Alltagspraxis auf der Grundlage wechselseitiger Verständigung und Vereinbarung abläuft und von Gewohnheiten, nicht von Befehlen geleitet wird." (Mumford, L. 1986)[33]

Mumford also describes the development towards megalomania, dogmatism and intolerance for other cultures, and is therefore not reserved for Western culture of the past two thousand years alone.
And Mumford also describes a source of "unreality".

"Gesunder Menschenverstand war das, was dem Königtum fast ex definitione fehlte: Wenn die Befehle des Königs ausgeführt waren, wagte keiner ihm offen zu sagen, wie sie sich ausgewirkt hatten. Mit der absoluten Macht, die die Königswürde verlieh, kamen Arroganz, Rücksichtslosigkeit, Starrheit, Zwang und Uneinsichtigkeit, wie keine kleine Gemeinschaft sie bei irgendeinem ihrer Angehörigen geduldet hätte – wiewohl man die aggressiven und unmenschlichen Eigenschaften, aus denen sich eine so ehrgeizige Führungsweise ergibt, überall antreffen

---

33   "The effectiveness of kingship throughout history is based on this very combination of the predatory bravery and leadership of the hunter with the astronomy and divine inspiration of the priest. In more primitive societies, these roles were long represented separately by a war chief and a peace chief. In both cases, the magical attributes of kingship were based on special functional aptitude - the willingness to bear responsibility and make leadership decisions. Leadership was supported by the priesthood, who observed natural phenomena and had the ability to interpret signs, gather knowledge and ensure the execution of orders.
The king claimed and received power over the life and death of the entire community. This way of establishing cooperation over a large area is in contrast to the modest ways of life of the farming village, whose everyday practice is based on mutual understanding and agreement and is guided by habits, not by orders." (Mumford, L. 1986)

kann, wie Margaret Mead bei den Mundugumors herausfand, deren Führer von der Gemeinschaft als »wirklich böse Männer«, als aggressiv und gierig nach Macht und Prestige angesehen werden. ... Allzu oft identifizierten sich, wie die Dokumente zeigen, die Beamten, die die Anordnungen des Königs ausführten, mit der Quelle der Autorität und übertrieben die königliche Arroganz, ohne sie durch königliche Gnade zu kompensieren." (Mumford, L. 1986)[34]

10.1   Ruler by the grace of God

The rulers, the emperors and kings, either declare themselves to be gods, or at least rulers by the grace of God, as if they had a direct mandate and legitimacy from God. In ancient Egypt they built pyramids for their dead bodies. In Western Europe they built their palaces, castles and palaces with the resources plundered from their citizens and foreign peoples. Not only are people robbed of their resources, but they are also brought into a relationship of dependency, as a basic pattern of narcissistic relationship structures.

---

34 "Common sense was what kingship lacked almost by definition: when the king's orders were carried out, no one dared to tell him openly how they had worked. With the absolute power that kingship conferred came arrogance, ruthlessness, rigidity, coercion and intransigence such as no small community would have tolerated in any of its members - although the aggressive and inhuman qualities that give rise to such ambitious leadership can be found everywhere, as Margaret Mead found among the Mundugumors, whose leaders are regarded by the community as "really bad men", aggressive and greedy for power and prestige. ... All too often, as the documents show, the officials who carried out the king's orders identified themselves with the source of authority and exaggerated royal arrogance without compensating it with royal grace." (Mumford, L. 1986)

10.2 God's representative on earth

On the one hand, it is the change from the collective nature myth of Judaism to the solipsistic relationship with God in Christianity that made it possible for people to appoint themselves as God's representatives.
And to impose this view on other people.
On the other hand, it is also the connection between church and state that creates the power complex.

"Es kann nicht wirklich überraschen, dass das Christentum Ciceros Würde in eine von Gott verliehene Menschenwürde umwandelt. Gott persönlich habe sie allen Menschen eingehaucht (Kath. Katechismus 1934), er sei „Krone der Schöpfung", gottebenbildlich und solle sich „die Erde untertan" machen (1 Moses 1,26 ff). Mit dem Anspruch, Gott habe jedem Menschen eine spezifische Würde eingehaucht, wird Ciceros Lehrmeinung aufgehoben, Würde werde vor allem durch eigenes Verhalten und durch das gegenüber der Gemeinschaft erworben. Zugleich wird die alles überragende Bindung des Menschen an Gott herausgestellt und damit sowohl die Bedeutung der Kirche als „Stellvertreterin Gottes" manifestiert, als auch ihr Mitspracherecht in allem, was das Menschenbild betrifft, gesichert. Diese Strategie hat fast zweitausend Jahre gewirkt und ist auch heute noch wirksam." (Bergmeier, R. 2018)[35]

---

35 "It is not really surprising that Christianity transforms Cicero's dignity into a human dignity bestowed by God. God personally breathed it into all people (Catholic Catechism 1934), he is the "crown of creation", made in God's image and should "subdue the earth" (Genesis 1:26 ff). The claim that God breathed a specific dignity into every human being repeals Cicero's doctrine that dignity is acquired primarily through one's own behavior and that towards the community. At the same time, the overriding bond of man to God is emphasized, thus manifesting both the importance of the church as "God's representative" and securing its right to have a say in everything that concerns the image of man. This strategy has worked for

The self-appointed representatives of God plundered the people just as emperors, kings and princes did. And they did this in order to build cathedrals and churches for themselves!

11 Incubation and infection

If the Cunctos Populos is identified as an infection of the Western world with the narcissism virus, the task of clarifying the incubation period and the course of infection remains.

The fact that the infection does not lead directly to the development of generalized symptoms, but only now, after about 1,600 years, to the "age of narcissism" (Lasch, Ch. 1980), is mainly due to the fact that the majority of the population did not have the necessary degrees of freedom for centuries, but lived in both material and emotional dependence, as "vassals". See the chapter "Narcissism must be affordable".

Narcissism thus remained limited to three small groups of people: the supposed representatives of God on earth, the rulers by the grace of God, and the philosophers who indulge in metaphysics.

„Philosophy thus boasting of its own impotence, is a tradition of that theological spirit which, terrified at the free exercise of Doubt, yet conscious of the necessity of Doubt for the activity of reason, excommunicated the Intellect as an heresiarch, after having vilified this life as a theatre for Satan. There was a time when all knowledge was considered dangerous, except for theologians and lawyers; for others it was of the nature of Magic. The tradition still lingers; and a vague horror hangs over all ‚prying into the mysteries of the universe.'"

---

almost two thousand years and is still effective today." (Bergmeier, R. 2018)

(Lewes, G. H. 1874)

„In this contempt of the actual in favour of the vaguely-imagi-
ned possible, this neglect of reality in favour of a supposed de-
eper reality, this disregard of light in the search for a light behind the light, metaphysicians have been led to seek the "thing
in itself" beyond the region of Experience. To reflective minds
it was early apparent that such a quaesitum was a phantom; and
because it could not be grasped, they declared,—not that this
phantom-essence was beyond our reach,—but that all essences
were impenetrable mysteries. With the reality before them they
declared it was a phantom, and that the shadow was the reality,
the essence." (Lewes, G. H. 1874)

„The philosopher looks away from the Visible and Actual, en-
deavouring to form a picture of the Invisible and Possible. He
strives to discover not what we should see with sharpened fa-
culties, but what would be seen were the constitution of things
different from that which it is. Philosophy is not an instrument
like the telescope or microscope, intended only to magnify the
powers of Sense, but an organon of Imagination by which to
reconstruct an ideal world of Abstraction."
(Lewes, G. H. 1874)

Western philosophy arose within the dogmatic boundaries of
Catholicism. And from this philosophy, in turn, psychology
emerged with the postulates of the culture-less, we-less and body-less I (Schmidt, B. 2020b).

„For a very long period philosophers deemed it enough to study Mind with little reference to its dependence on the Organism; the introspection of Consciousness was supposed to be
sufficient. Nay, even when Physiology began to furnish indica-

tions of the connection between vital and psychical phenomena, and to exhibit the dependence of mental states on neural states, the psychologists pointed to the fact that Consciousness told us nothing of such dependence; and hence they concluded that Psychology, occupied solely with Consciousness and its changes, need not concern itself with Physiology and its laws. Indeed Psychology without illumination from Biology is something like the Astronomy of the Chaldeans without the aid of Mathematics; watching the stars however patiently would no more disclose the laws of their movement, than watching the changes in Consciousness would disclose their laws. Not only were centuries of such observation inadequate, but we now know that some of the elementary facts escaped notice, and must for ever have escaped it unless otherwise aided." (Lewes, G. H. 1874)[36]

11.1   Development of "unreality"

For Catholicism as well as Christianity, unreality is a central basis. It is the belief in a paradise, a life after death, which is of the greatest importance. It is not the life here that counts, but rather it only offers the way to paradise with eternal life - or to hell with eternal damnation. It is not reality itself that is important, but rather it is only a reference to paradise.[37]. Reality is interpreted as having been created by God according to the "ordo rationis", with man as the centre, on his way back to God.

„Von Gott gehen alle Geschöpfe aus und kehren je auf ihre Art durch Verähnlichung zu ihm zurück – zu dem

---

36   It is to a large extent both the statements of G. H. Lewes, as well as the ignoring of them by psychology, that convinced me of the necessity of developing a new scientific psychonomy.

37   For the cultural-historical development of this idea see e.g. Wundt, Wilhelm (1913) "Elements of Folk Psychology".

einen Endzweck, dass in ihrer Mitte das eine Geschöpf,
der Mensch, zum vollen Ebenbild Gottes wird."
(Pesch 1988, zitiert nach Schmidt 2015)[38]

But even if the afterlife was taught as a goal by the church, the
majority of people were confronted with the reality of this
world on a daily basis, with the struggle for survival.
It is only the developments of the last two hundred years that
have led to the expansion of "unreality", i.e. the detachment
from reality. The developments within science, technology and
medicine. And these in connection with increasing urbanization
and the "democratization of the irrational" (Chapter 5.3).

"Bis zur gegenwärtigen Periode der Urbanisierung lebte die
Mehrzahl der Weltbevölkerung, wie der französische Geograph
Max Sorre hervorhob etwa vier Fünftel zu seiner Zeit -, immer
noch in Dörfern und führte von der Geburt bis zum Tode eine
Lebensweise, die der uralten neolithischen Form in allem außer
dem Gebrauch von Steinwerkzeugen weitgehend glich. Selbst
unter den neuen Universalreligionen (wie dem Christentum)
blieben die alten Haus- und Schreingötter und Dämonen bestehen, in Italien und Frankreich ebenso wie in Mexiko, Java und
China. Die außerordentliche Beständigkeit der neolithischen
Dorfkultur im Vergleich zu den kühneren Veränderungen der
späteren städtischen Zivilisationen zeugt davon, daß sie den natürlichen Bedingungen und den Fähigkeiten des Menschen besser gerecht wurde als jede dynamischere, aber weniger ausge-
wogene Kultur." (Mumford, L. 1986)[39]

---

38   "All creatures come from God and return to him in their own way through
     similarity – with the one final goal that in their midst the one creature,
     man, becomes the full image of God." (Pesch 1988, quoted in Schmidt
     2015)

39   "Until the present period of urbanization, the majority of the world's po-
     pulation - as the French geographer Max Sorre pointed out - about four-

However, Mumford overlooks the significance of Catholicism as the realization of the power complex that he himself described for other cultures, i.e. the connection between state and church. And he also overlooks the self-deification, which was initially limited to a small group. But it is true that the majority of people lived in rather modest conditions in the countryside, usually in material dependence on their princes and feudal lords. And in emotional dependence on the self-proclaimed mother church.

"Immer drehte sich die weißhäutige Menschheit um ein einziges *ens generalissimum*, genannt „Gott".
Dieser „Gott" wohnte unsichtbar hinter heuchel-logischen Systemen, hinter heuchel-moralischen Ordnungen. Keiner durfte ihn sehn, keiner ihn nennen. Wir aber reißen todbereit den letzten Schleier von seinem Bilde. Und was erblicken wir? Uns Selbst." (Lessing, Th. 1929/2021)[40]

---

fifths in his time - still lived in villages and led from birth to death a way of life that closely resembled the ancient Neolithic form in everything except the use of stone tools. Even under the new universal religions (such as Christianity) the old household and shrine gods and demons persisted, in Italy and France as well as in Mexico, Java and China.
The extraordinary persistence of the Neolithic village culture in comparison with the bolder changes of later urban civilizations testifies to the fact that it was better adapted to natural conditions and human capabilities than any more dynamic but less balanced culture." (Mumford, L. 1986)

40 "White-skinned humanity always revolved around a single ens generalissimum, called "God".
This "God" lived invisibly behind hypocritical logical systems, behind hypocritical moral orders. No one was allowed to see him, no one was allowed to name him. But we, ready to die, tear the last veil from his image. And what do we see? Ourselves." (Lessing, Th. 1929/2021)

11.2 "Missionary work"

The missionizing of "poor heathens," the forced conversion of heretics, is the rabid behavior of the classes infected with the narcissism virus.

Under the pretext of missionizing, those of different faiths are fought and people are brought into material and emotional dependence.

> "'*Mission unter den Heiden, das ist Dienst*
> *an der Seele: das ist Europas rettende Liebe.'*
> *Johann Hinrich Wichern.*

Die Rettende Liebe, in deren Namen 20.000 Hexen verbrannt, 200.000 Ketzer zum Tode geführt, 200.000 Juden gefoltert wurden, die Bartholomäusnacht gefeiert, Montezuma von Mexiko auf den glühenden Rost gelegt, Afrika verunrechtet, Indien unterjocht wurde, die Rettende Liebe schickt sich an, über die Erde hin die frohe Botschaft zu verbreiten:

'Es gibt nur einen Gott: das menschliche Ich, und Mammon ist sein Profet.'" (Lessing, Th. 1929/2021)[41]

Thus, narcissistic pseudo-empathy in the form of "missionary work" did not serve to save souls, but to justify crusades and colonization. In this way, the entire earth was brought into contact with the narcissism virus.

---

41 "'*Mission among the heathens, that is service to the soul: that is Europe's saving love.' Johann Hinrich Wichern.*
The saving love, in whose name 20,000 witches were burned, 200,000 heretics were put to death, 200,000 Jews were tortured, St. Bartholomew's Day was celebrated, Montezuma of Mexico was laid on the red-hot gridiron, Africa was violated, India was subjugated, the saving love is preparing to spread the good news across the earth:
'There is only one God: the human ego, and Mammon is his prophet.'"
(Lessing, Th. 1929/2021)

On both points, the Crusades and colonization, I would like to let Theodor Lessing speak.

11.2.a Crusades

"Im Jahre 1096 begann der erste jener sieben das Morgenland ausräubernden Verbrecherzüge. 300.000 abenteuerlustige Tunichtgute und Habenichtse mit hohen Titeln und Namen taten sich zusammen unter Gottfrieds von Bouillon raubritterlicher Führung, um „den armen heidnischen Erdenkindern die gute Botschaft der christlichen Erlösung zu bringen".
Grenzenlose, kaum vorstellbare Martern, wahre Taumelfeste des Massen-, Klassen- und Rassenhasses haben diese von allen Zaubern der Poesie umspielten Mord- und Raubfahrereien über die unglückselige Menschheit gebracht."
(Lessing, Th. 1929/2021)[42]

11.2.b Colonization and exploitation

"Kein Angehöriger der weißhäutigen Rasse wird jemals glauben, daß Kolonisation einzig stattgefunden habe, „um Naturvölkern die Segnungen der Kultur zu bringen", noch auch, daß die Missionsarbeit von den christlichen Kirchen ausging, einzig in der Absicht: „die armen Seelen zu retten".
Mission und Kolonisation sind Formen des Imperialismus:

---

[42] "In 1096, the first of those seven criminal campaigns that plundered the Orient began. 300,000 adventurous ne'er-do-wells and have-nots with high titles and names joined forces under the robber-knight leadership of Godfrey of Bouillon to "bring the good news of Christian salvation to the poor pagan children of the earth."
Boundless, almost unimaginable tortures, true frenzy of mass, class and racial hatred, have been brought upon unfortunate humanity by these murder and robbery campaigns, surrounded by all the magic of poetry."
(Lessing, Th. 1929/2021)

also eines Strebens nach Ausdehnung und nach Landbesitz."
(Lessing, Th. 1929/2021)[43]

Through looting, not only are those who have been robbed made materially dependent, but the means are also obtained to build even larger churches and cathedrals, castles, fortresses and palaces – without any sense of wrongdoing.

"Kaum sind die letzten Araber 1492 abgezogen, vereinen sich Kirche und König zur Ausplünderung der südamerikanischen Okkupationen. Indios werden gezwungen, aus Bergwerken das Gold und Silber herauszuholen, das zum Bau prachtvoller Paläste und Klöster benötigt wird. So wird beispielsweise in Portugal zwischen 1711 und 1730 das Großkloster Mafra zu Ehren des hl. Antonius von Padua geschaffen. An dem 38.000 Quadratmeter großen Bau mit 1200 Räumen sind bis zu 50.000 Arbeitskräfte eingesetzt, die unter großen Mühen und 1400 Todesopfern und unter der Aufsicht von 7000 Soldaten das Monumentalbauwerk für 330 Mönche schaffen."
(Bergmeier, R. 2018)[44]

---

43 "No member of the white-skinned race will ever believe that colonization took place solely "to bring the blessings of culture to indigenous peoples," nor that missionary work was undertaken by the Christian churches with the sole intention of "saving the poor souls." Mission and colonization are forms of imperialism: that is, a striving for expansion and land ownership." (Lessing, Th. 1929/2021)

44 "As soon as the last Arabs had left in 1492, the church and the king joined forces to plunder the South American occupations. Indians were forced to extract the gold and silver from mines that were needed to build magnificent palaces and monasteries. In Portugal, for example, the Great Monastery of Mafra was built between 1711 and 1730 in honor of St. Anthony of Padua. Up to 50,000 workers were employed on the 38,000 square meter building with 1,200 rooms, who created the monumental building for 330 monks with great effort and 1,400 deaths and under the supervision of 7,000 soldiers." (Bergmeier, R. 2018)

11.2.c Contagion

It is the campaigns of plunder and destruction that rob the indigenous inhabitants of their possessions and their gods, force them into material and emotional dependence, and destroy traditional cultures, making people susceptible to the rabies virus of narcissism.

"Die durch Mission und Kolonisation in ihrem Wachstum geknickten Völker wandeln sich in leidenschaftliche Anbeter der Ideologie ihrer Unterdrücker. Die Kolonisatoren dagegen werden zu wissenschaftlichen Liebhabern der alten Bräuche, Landessitten, Sagen und Mythen, welche die Forscher im Abendlande längst besser kennen und tiefer begreifen als die im Sinne der Betriebsmenschheit noch primitiven Völker selber."
(Lessing, Th. 1929/2021)[45]

12 Consequences

"Es läßt sich leicht zeigen, daß diese Theologie– (» Religion« bedarf durchaus keiner Theologie und am allerwenigsten eines »Dasein Gottes«)– insgeheim ein einziger Idiomorphismus ist. Es dreht sich immer und ewig um das Ich."
(Lessing, Th. 1930)[46]

---

[45] "The peoples whose growth has been stunted by mission and colonization are transformed into passionate worshippers of the ideology of their oppressors. The colonizers, on the other hand, become scientific lovers of the old customs, local traditions, legends and myths, which researchers in the West have long known better and understood more deeply than the peoples themselves, who are still primitive in the sense of industrial humanity." (Lessing, Th. 1929/2021)

[46] "It is easy to show that this theology – ("religion" does not require any theology and least of all an "existence of God") – is secretly a single idiomorphism. It always and forever revolves around the self." (Lessing, Th. 1930)

And this I must necessarily be defined as a solipsistic I, without culture, body and we.

As an I created by God, which develops from within itself, from a Bleuler-like autism into a social world.

The dogma of the solipsistic I still shapes our psyche and Western psychology, our pedagogy as well as our self-image, in kindergartens and schools... in the separation of the humanities and natural sciences.

If, for example, constructivism is accused of solipsism, then this is not inherent in constructivism, but already in the postulates underlying our self-image.

If the social constructivists rightly point out that we individually construct our *social reality*, then they are right. But they overlook the fact that, above all, and from the very first breath, *we construct our reality socially.*

The problem is not that this has not already been recognized in some areas, but never in the overall view. This is put together below from the existing mosaic pieces.

12.1   We-, body- and culture-less I

It is the threefold dogma of a solipsistic self that is independent of the body, social environment and the cultural development of this environment that has so far stood in the way of understanding the human psyche.

These three dogmas have led to a state that is comparable to a box with three different locks.

Although a number of researchers have opened one or the other, sometimes even two locks at the same time, i.e. the social conditioning of the self, its dependence on the cultural development of the environment, etc. But opening all three locks at the same time, i.e. eliminating all three dogmas and thus "opening the box", has not yet been achieved.

The criticism of mainstream psychology, its methods and its methodology, as repeatedly presented by Jaan Valsiner, Aaro Toomela and others, is correct, but has not yet led to the dissolution of the existing dogmas. The cultural psychology represented by those mentioned, as effective as some of its findings are, only opens one of the three locks and therefore remains trapped in the box of Catholic dogmas.

Thus, the dogmas described here were able to persist, while at the same time essential findings, such as the existence of "psychonomic species," remained limited.

"Und so verkehrten sich die Pole: Bewußtsein, Logos, Geist wurden zum wahren Leben. Und das tragende Element gewann den Charakter eines dunklen Abfalls vom Geiste und seiner göttlichen Reinheit.

Das ist der Dünkel, welcher Kant sprechen ließ: »Der Verstand erschafft die Natur«, und welcher Hegel höhnen ließ: »Wenn die Natur nicht mit der Vernunft übereinstimmt, um so schlimmer für die Natur.«" (Lessing, Th. 1930)[47]

„In der zweiten Hälfte der Patristik (vom Konzil zu Nikäa 325 bis zu Karl d. Gr. 800) ist „Gott" bereits geworden zum „Entwerdungsvorgang des Geistes, welcher im Haupte des Menschen aus den Gefängnissen der Materie Sich selbst entkerkert". (Lessing, Th. 1929/2021)[48]

---

47   "And so the poles reversed: consciousness, logos, spirit became true life. And the supporting element took on the character of a dark apostasy from the spirit and its divine purity.
This is the conceit that made Kant say: "The understanding creates nature," and that made Hegel sneer: "If nature does not agree with reason, so much the worse for nature."" (Lessing, Th. 1930)

48   "In the second half of the Patristic period (from the Council of Nicaea in 325 to Charlemagne in 800), "God" had already become the "process of depersonalization of the spirit, which in the head of man frees itself from the prisons of matter." (Lessing, Th. 1929/2021)

The we-, body- and culture-less I is the epitome of the narcissistic I, which believes itself to be independent and therefore necessarily and dogmatically defines itself as independent of any environment, be it social, cultural or physical.

Body-less

"Wenn der Körper das Selbst ist, muß das wirkliche Selbstbild ein körperliches Bild sein. Man kann das wirkliche Selbstbild nur abschaffen, indem man die Realität eines verkörperten Selbst leugnet. Narzißtische Menschen leugnen nicht, daß sie einen Körper haben. So schwach ist ihr Realitätssinn nicht. Aber sie sehen den Körper als Werkzeug des Geistes an, ihrem Willen unterworfen. Er funktioniert nur gemäß ihren Vorstellungen, ohne Gefühl. Obwohl der Körper wirksam als Werkzeug funktionieren und wie eine Maschine Leistungen erbringen oder einem wie eine Statue vorkommen kann, fehlt es ihm dann an »Leben«, Und gerade dieses Gefühl der Lebendigkeit läßt die Erfahrung des Selbst entstehen." (Lowen, A. 1992)[49]

We-less

"Der Soziologe Norbert Elias hat zu Recht festgestellt, daß in den europäischen Gesellschaften seit der Renaissance die Idee des Menschen von seiner Vereinzelung, von der Abschließung des eigenen Inneren gegenüber allem, was draußen ist, bestimmt worden ist. In der philosophisch-soziologischen Traditi-

---

49 "If the body is the self, the real self-image must be a physical image. One can only abolish the real self-image by denying the reality of an embodied self. Narcissistic people do not deny that they have a body. Their sense of reality is not that weak. But they see the body as a tool of the mind, subject to their will. It functions only according to their ideas, without feeling. Although the body can function effectively as a tool and perform like a machine or appear like a statue, it lacks "life". And it is precisely this feeling of aliveness that gives rise to the experience of the self." (Lowen, A. 1992)

on gibt es, wie Elias darlegt, kaum einen Denkansatz, bei dem man grundsätzlich von einer Vielzahl aufeinander angewiesener Menschen ausgeht. «Im Mittelpunkt des menschlichen Universums, so erschien es von nun an, steht jeder einzelne Mensch für sich als ein von allen anderen letzten Endes völlig unabhängiges Individuum.» Die Gesellschaft stellt sich von diesem Ausgangspunkt aus als ein Haufen total vereinzelter Menschen dar, «deren eigentliches Wesen in ihrem Inneren verschlossen ist und die daher allenfalls äußerlich und von der Oberfläche her miteinander kommunizieren». Daher komme der Begriff des Individuums, das außerhalb der Gesellschaft, und der Begriff der Gesellschaft, die außerhalb des Individuums existiere." (Richter, H. E. 1979)[50]

But the dogma of the we-less I has existed, as already explained, since the beginning of the Christian faith and not just since the Renaissance. In this sense, the majority of Western European metaphysical philosophy is also the expression of a narcissistic personality that has fled from reality into the ivory tower[51].

---

50 "The sociologist Norbert Elias has rightly stated that in European societies since the Renaissance, the idea of man has been determined by his isolation, by the closure of his own inner being from everything that is outside. In the philosophical-sociological tradition, as Elias explains, there is hardly any approach to thinking that fundamentally assumes a large number of people who are dependent on one another. «At the centre of the human universe, it seemed from now on, each individual stands for himself as an individual who is ultimately completely independent of all others.» From this starting point, society presents itself as a bunch of totally isolated people, «whose true essence is locked away within themselves and who therefore communicate with one another at best externally and superficially.» Hence the concept of the individual, who exists outside of society, and the concept of society, which exists outside of the individual.» (Richter, H. E. 1979)

51 See e.g. Lewes, G. H. (1874): Problems of Life and Mind

Development from the inside out

One consequence of the dogmas is the false idea of a "true self" that develops from the inside outwards, as can be found in the early Piaget, among others. It is the idea of a "true self" that can be found in many parts of psychology and especially psychotherapy.

At the beginning of the 20th century, Lev Vygotsky opposed this position, represented primarily by Piaget, of a ego that develops linearly from the inside outwards and is thus largely fixed, in three ways. Firstly, he shows, and this is especially true of language development, that development proceeds in the opposite direction - from the outside inwards. That the child communicates with the environment as a social being from the very beginning.

Vygotsky also shows that this development is by no means linear, but rather through metamorphoses and crises.

And thirdly, that the child's development is shaped by the cultural environment, which itself is subject to historical development.

Cultur-less

One of the most widespread misconceptions, especially in anthropology, is that the "mind sets" of the Neanderthals were the same as ours. This misconception is based on the assumption that one's own self, one's own thinking, develops within a culture but remains largely unaffected by it. The respective culture only forms the framework and the possibilities through the accumulated cultural assets.

In contrast to this, however, Vygotsky together with Luria show, based on studies in Russian regions that were on the threshold of literacy (Vygotsky, L.S.; Luria, A.R. 1993 "Studies on the History of Behavior"), that it is not only people who shape culture, but that culturally developed tools such as writing and numbers have a feedback effect on human thinking. That "mind sets" therefore change due to cultural tools.

12.1.a Science

I have already explained the effects of the development of the sciences shaped by Catholicism in the "Entwurf einer wissenschaftlichen Psychologie" (Schmidt, B. 2020b). As already mentioned here, these are primarily
• the division into body and mind, and the resulting division into humanities and natural sciences,
• but also the dualism that underlies our thinking alone (!).
• And the idea of reward and punishment that is effective in many areas, although it is actually a matter of the "negotiation of meaning" (Wenger, Etienne 1998)[52].
It is precisely this negotiation that is important and leads to the formation of societies and to children growing up in these societies. A negotiation that can also seduce people within a culture so that, despite enlightenment and a high level of education, they believe that men in funny clothes are the representatives of a god on earth.

"Ich glaube nun mit dem hier vorliegenden Werke ein für allemal klar bewiesen zu haben, daß der ganze Geschichtsvorgang, den wir in Europa und Amerika „Fortschritt" oder ‚Zivilisation' nennen, ja daß die gesamte Menschwerdung der Erde steht und fällt mit dem Christentum. Wir werden uns also fürder nicht mehr täuschen lassen durch den Umstand, daß die christlichen Kirchen dem Prozeß des wissenschaftlichen und sittlichen Fortschritts hier oder dort zu widerstreben scheinen. Dieser Fortschritt, auch dort wo er sich gegen christliche Theologie

---

52 See e.g. Schmidt, B.J. (2020a): DOGmatismus. Neue Perspektiven auf Mensch, Hund und Kultur.

oder Kirche kehrt, ist durchaus nur das Ergebnis und die folge-
rechte Verwirklichung der christlichen Kirche und ihrer Gottes-
lehre. Christentum ist Übermächtigung der Natur durch den
zielgerichteten Menschen." (Lessing, Th. 1929/2021)[53]

Here, too, it should be pointed out once again that Lessing is
mistaken in that this is not about Christianity, but about the Catholicism of Western Europe.
Furthermore, it is the ideological (ideology as an "exclusive
promise of salvation" - see Schmidt, B.; Ganz, A. 2017) devaluation of reality based on the dogma of an afterlife with eternal life.
Dogmatic belief is in contradiction to science.

„Ancient formulas and time-honoured creeds are yielding as
much to internal pressure as to external assault. The expansion
of knowledge is loosening the very earth clutched by the roots
of creeds and churches." (Lewes, G. H. 1874)

But above all, it is also the turning away from reality in favor
of a supposed afterlife.
Life and consciousness are no longer seen as miracles, but as
God's creation.
Miracles are now performed by people. And the miracle wor-
kers are declared saints.

---

53   "I believe that with this work I have now clearly demonstrated once and
     for all that the entire historical process that we in Europe and America call
     'progress' or 'civilization', indeed that the entire humanization of the
     earth stands and falls with Christianity. We will therefore no longer allow
     ourselves to be deceived by the fact that the Christian churches here or
     there seem to resist the process of scientific and moral progress. This pro-
     gress, even where it turns against Christian theology or church, is absolu-
     tely only the result and the logical realization of the Christian church and
     its doctrine of God. Christianity is the overpowering of nature by goal-
     oriented man." (Lessing, Th. 1929/2021)

The highest value is attributed to the martyrs who despise real, current life in favor of a life in paradise.

Man declares himself to be the image of God created by God, separates himself from nature in all its facets. Separates himself from the environment and culture.

He ascribes the rational soul to himself alone.

Measure and middle are lost through the dualism of heaven and hell, good and evil.

Kant's demand to treat people not only as means, but always as ends in themselves, becomes an either/or.

The exploitation of animate and inanimate nature is the consequence of the fact that they are only seen as means. Even by those who claim to see them only as ends in themselves (see Schmidt, B.J. 2022).

The knowledge of enantiodromy is lost.

12.2   "Mutual Aid" (Kropotkin) becomes charity

The mutual aid that Kropotkin (1902) describes as an essential factor in evolution becomes a one-sided charity. The charity of the Lord towards his dependent subjects, the church towards the believers.

A charity of power imbalance and pseudo-empathy. Along with the appreciation of the charitable and the devaluation of the needy, who should be kept as dependent as possible. A charity that opens the door to abuse and mistreatment (Schmidt, B. 2022).

Here we should at least briefly point out the parallels to all the charitable institutions in the care of the disabled, which lock their charges in cages, if in golden ones. When Lev Vygotsky repeatedly calls in his writings for the Germans to free their special schools from the spirit of charity, I can only agree with him.

"Von dem Zeitpunkt jedoch, wo der Mensch das Hirtenamt übernahm und der zu Mensch gewordene Gott ihm die Erde anvertraute, da wandelte sich die Beziehung zur Natur in falschgefühlige Fürsorge, für welche kennzeichnend ist das biblische Wort: „Der Gerechte erbarmt sich seines Viehs", darinnen derselbe Hochmut steckt wie in jeder Forderung von Mitleid, Erbarmen, Duldung oder Toleranz – geistige Zustände, welche erst dort Platz greifen, wo Gemeinschaft und Liebe eben ermangeln.

Aus welchen Beweggründen etwa übernimmt der „gute Hirte" die Bevormundung seiner Herde? Er will sie erst scheren und sodann fressen." (Lessing, Th. 1929/2021)[54]

I would like to let Kropotkin have his say for further explanation:

"When the Mutual Aid institutions — the tribe, the village community, the guilds, the medieval city — began, in the course of history, to lose their primitive character, to be invaded by parasitic growths, and thus to become hindrances to progress, the revolt of individuals against these institutions took always two different aspects. Part of those who rose up strove to purify the old institutions, or to work out a higher form of commonwealth, based upon the same Mutual Aid principles; they tried,

---

54 "However, from the moment when man took over the office of shepherd and God, who had become man, entrusted him with the earth, the relationship with nature changed into a falsely sensitive care, which is characterized by the biblical saying: "The righteous man has mercy on his cattle," which contains the same arrogance as in every demand for compassion, mercy, forbearance or tolerance - spiritual states that only take hold where community and love are lacking.

For what motives, for example, does the "good shepherd" take on the guardianship of his flock? He wants to shear them first and then eat them." (Lessing, Th. 1929/2021)

for instance, to introduce the principle of "compensation," instead of the lex talionis, and later on, the pardon of offences, or a still higher ideal of equality before the human conscience, in lieu of "compensation," according to class - value. But at the very same time, another portion of the same individual rebels endeavoured to break down the protective institutions of mutual support, with no other intention but to increase their own wealth and their own powers. In this three-cornered contest, between the two classes of revolted individuals and the supporters of what existed, lies the real tragedy of history."
(Kropotkin, P. 1902)

"The students of Roman law and the prelates of the Church, closely bound together since the time of Innocent the Third, had succeeded in paralyzing the idea — the antique Greek idea — which presided at the foundation of the cities. For two or three hundred years they taught from the pulpit, the University chair, and the judges' bench, that salvation must be sought for in a strongly-centralized State, placed under a semi-divine authority; that one man can and must be the saviour of society, and that in the name of public salvation he can commit any violence: burn men and women at the stake, make them perish under indescribable tortures, plunge whole provinces into the most abject misery. Nor did they fail to give object lessons to this effect on a grand scale, and with an unheard-of cruelty, wherever the king's sword and the Church's fire, or both at once, could reach. By these teachings and examples, continually repeated and enforced upon public attention, the very minds of the citizens had been shaped into a new mould. They began to find no authority too extensive, no killing by degrees too cruel, once it was "for public safety." (Kropotkin, P. 1902)

"The absorption of all social functions by the State necessarily favoured the development of an unbridled, narrow-minded individualism." (Kropotkin, P. 1902)

But ultimately, one must assume an interaction between the individualism already shaped by Catholicism and state power. It was only the change from the collective nature myth of Jewish origin to the solipsistic divine creation of Christianity that paved the way for further developments, and these were consolidated by the power complex of Catholicism.

"The result is, that the theory which maintains that men can, and must, seek their own happiness in a disregard of other people's wants is now triumphant all round in law, in science, in religion. It is the religion of the day, and to doubt of its efficacy is to be a dangerous Utopian. Science loudly proclaims that the struggle of each against all is the leading principle of nature, and of human societies as well. To that struggle Biology ascribes the progressive evolution of the animal world. History takes the same line of argument ; and political economists, in their naive ignorance, trace all progress of modern industry and machinery to the "wonderful" effects of the same principle. The very religion of the pulpit is a religion of individualism, slightly mitigated by more or less charitable relations to one's neighbours, chiefly on Sundays. "Practical" men and theorists, men of science and religious preachers, lawyers and politicians, all agree upon one thing — that individualism may be more or less softened in its harshest effects by charity, but that it is the only secure basis for the maintenance of society and its ulterior progress." (Kropotkin, P. 1902)

And Bergmeier will also have his say once again, who aptly explains the term *pseudo-empathy* that I coined (Schmidt, B. 2022).

„Wahr ist, dass der deutsche Katholizismus als staatlich legiti-mierte und subventionierte „Körperschaft des öffentlichen Rechts" (!) das Gegenteil von dem ist, was in den Evangelien als eigenständige Gemeinden mit urdemokratischer Verfassung zur Pflege der wahren Tugenden Christi beschrieben wird. Und es kann dem Christen seinen Glauben verleiden, wenn er hört, dass das Kölner Bistum auf einem *Milliardenvermögen* sitzt, die Hälfte der Kölner Haupteinkaufsstraße besitzt und gleich-zeitig mit der Arroganz der Wohlgenährten zum Opfer für die Armen auffordert, ohne auch nur ein Grundstück zu verkau-fen." (Bergmeier, R. 2018)[55]

It is the bitter and at the same time unavoidable realization that the "culturally camouflaged predatory apes" (Theodor Lessing) were only US. And WE spread this virus across the earth.

12.3   Virtue Becomes Morality

One of the central errors of Western self-perception is the claim of unbroken continuity from ancient Greece, both philosophi-cally and politically, to the present day. This overlooks the cen-turies that existed far from any democracy and were shaped so-

---

[55]   "It is true that German Catholicism, as a state-legitimized and subsidized "corporation under public law" (!), is the opposite of what is described in the Gospels as independent communities with a fundamentally democra-tic constitution to cultivate the true virtues of Christ. And it can spoil the Christian's faith when he hears that the Cologne diocese sits on billions of dollars in assets, owns half of Cologne's main shopping street and at the same time, with the arrogance of the well-fed, calls for sacrifices for the poor without selling a single piece of land." (Bergmeier, R. 2018)

lely by Catholicism. And when the classical texts of the Greek philosophers found their way back to Western Europe in the Middle Ages, it was under the conditions of the Church[56].

With regard to narcissism as the rabies of Western culture, the change from Greek virtue to Catholic morality is of particular importance. And even though a doctrine of virtue was again developed in the Middle Ages on the basis of ancient philosophy, it did not prevail[57].

If virtue is aimed at one's own person, at its realization in a non-esoteric sense, morality is always aimed at others. Morality is always a double standard that dictates to others what one does not do oneself.

Morality offers the justification for bullying and harassing other people and forcing one's own ideas on them. Both, as will be shown, are both characteristics of narcissism and popular activities of narcissists.

Morality is always based on the narcissistic illusion of one's own moral superiority.

What is natural and therefore unavoidable is presented as immoral - for example, sexuality.

In this way, people are turned into sinners and at the same time offered indulgence for the sins they have created themselves.

13   Symptom development

Although infected with the narcissism virus by the Cunctos Populos and spread by the crusades and colonizations justified as missionary work, the development of narcissistic symptoms remained limited to small groups. However, all of the parts of

---

56   See Schmidt, B. (2020b): Entwurf einer wissenschaftlichen Psychologie.

57   On the virtue of ancient Greece, see, for example, H. D. F. Kitto's "Die Griechen. Von der Wirklichkeit eines geschichtlichen Vorbilds", and on the medieval doctrine of the four cardinal virtues "prudence, justice, courage, temperance" see the book by Josef Pieper "Das Viergespann".

the symptom complex mentioned at the beginning can be found in these groups.

The development towards the "age of narcissism" (Lasch, Ch. 1980) only began with the dissolution of the Neolithic way of life that had been stable for centuries.

This dissolution was necessary, but in no way sufficient. It was a first step towards the "democratization of the irrational" and towards the prosperity that is needed to be able to afford narcissism and its "unreality" at all.

13.1   Neolithic way of life

Until the 19th century, the vast majority of the population lived in rural areas, mostly illiterate and dependent on feudal lords. But they also had a direct connection to nature, and thus also received direct feedback on successes and mistakes. The "unreality" inherent in narcissism, the ignoring of reality, would, in case of doubt, result in immediate death.

"Die Verstädterung hat in den letzten 200 Jahren rapide zugenommen. In Deutschland ging die Landbevölkerung zwischen 1800 und 1925 von 75 Prozent auf 22,8 Prozent zurück. 1982 betrug ihr Anteil 15,4 Prozent. Ähnliche Entwicklungen zeichnen sich in anderen Industriestaaten, aber auch in den Entwicklungsländern ab." (Eibl-Eibesfeldt, I. 2004)[58]

These village communities certainly had their disadvantages, and glorifying the past is in no way justified. However, the ef-

---

58   "Urbanization has increased rapidly over the last 200 years. In Germany, the rural population fell from 75 percent to 22.8 percent between 1800 and 1925. In 1982, it was 15.4 percent. Similar developments are emerging in other industrialized countries, but also in developing countries." (Eibl-Eibesfeldt, I. 2004)

fect of these small units was very limited, and the degree of personal freedom was very restricted.

"Kurz, die neolithische Dorfgemeinschaft hatte für ihren Erfolg zu zahlen: Sie war eine Gefangene ihrer eigenen Tugenden. Der Horizont war zu eng, die Routine zu beschränkt, die Religion allzu stark an kleine Ahnengottheiten gebunden, das Dorf allzu selbstgefällig in seiner Isolierung, zu narzißtisch auf sich selbst bezogen, zu mißtrauisch dem Fremdling gegenüber, zu ablehnend gegen neue Bräuche – das eigene kleine Gute ein halsstarriger Feind des fremden Besten. Sogar die Sprache solcher Dörfer tendierte zur Inzucht, so daß manch ein lokaler Dialekt einen Tagesmarsch weiter kaum noch verständlich war. In überlebenden Stammesgemeinschaften versteinerten diese Fehler im Lauf fünftausendjähriger Wiederholung schützender Isolierung und perverser Vervollkommnung; das schöpferische Moment ist längst verschwunden.
Alle diese Wesenszüge tendierten zu Beharrung und Dauer – aber auf niedrigem Niveau. Einmal entwickelt, verlor die neolithische Kultur gerade die Eigenschaften, die sie anfangs so attraktiv gemacht hatten – ihre forschende Neugierde und ihre kühne Experimentierlust." (Mumford, L. 1986)[59]

---

59 "In short, the Neolithic village community had to pay for its success: it was a prisoner of its own virtues. The horizon was too narrow, the routine too limited, religion too closely tied to small ancestral deities, the village too complacent in its isolation, too narcissistic in its own right, too suspicious of the stranger, too hostile to new customs - its own little good a stubborn enemy of the foreign best. Even the language of such villages tended towards inbreeding, so that many a local dialect was barely understandable a day's march away. In surviving tribal communities these errors fossilized in the course of five thousand years of repetition of protective isolation and perverse perfection; the creative moment has long since disappeared.
All these traits tended towards persistence and permanence - but at a low level. Once developed, the Neolithic culture lost the very qualities that

The separation from village communities associated with the urbanization of the way of life gave people individual degrees of freedom on the one hand, but also a certain disorientation on the other.

In addition, there were social processes that led to further freedoms, for example through revolutions and uprisings.

13.2　Increasing degrees of freedom I

The degrees of freedom that Lasch, Wolfe and Tyler, among others, discuss for the 20th century and believe to be the cause of the spread of narcissism have been developing since the middle of the 19th century.

But it is the upheavals and changes of the 19th century that lead to new degrees of freedom and, above all, to a "democratization of the irrational."

13.3　Democratization of the Irrational

The democratization of the irrational, that is, the unbridled spread of dogmas and ideologies that had previously been the preserve of the church and secular rulers, took place in at least three areas: through the abolition of the Inquisition, the feudal system and censorship.

13.3.a　Inquisition

The essential changes towards our democratic-liberal self-image are not nearly as far back as we like to assume. This applies to the abolition of slavery (USA 1865, worldwide 1926

---

had made it so attractive in the first place - its inquiring curiosity and its bold desire to experiment." (Mumford, L. 1986)

and 1948), the introduction of the right to vote for women
(Germany 1918), as well as the abolition of the Inquisition.

"Wie keine zweite Institution verkörperte die "Spanische Inquisition" die Brutalität des katholischen Alleinvertretungsanspru-
ches. Die letzte von der Heiligen Inquisition angeklagte Person
wird am 7. November 1781 auf dem Scheiterhaufen verbrannt.
Es ist Beata von Salamanca. Ihr wird vorgeworfen, mit dem
Abgesandten der Hölle, dessen Pesthauch jeden durchfahrt,
paktiert zu haben. Noch im Jahre 1820 werden in den Inquisiti-
onskerkern von Madrid 21 Gefangene gefunden, die zum Teil
seit Jahren auf ihre Hinrichtung warten. Nicht einer von ihnen
kennt den Namen der Stadt, keiner weiß genau, was man ihm
vorwirft. Einer der Befreiten sollte am nächsten Tag hingerich-
tet werden." (Bergmeier, R. 2018)[60]

13.3.b   Feudal system

The abolition of the feudal system, which lasted for decades
during the 19th century, also meant that material dependence
on the landowners, i.e. princes, churches and monasteries, was
lost, at least for the time being. However, this dependence was
subsequently often exchanged for material dependence on the
factory owners, the new moneyed aristocracy.

---

60   "Like no other institution, the "Spanish Inquisition" embodied the brutali-
ty of the Catholic claim to sole representation. The last person accused by
the Holy Inquisition was burned at the stake on November 7, 1781. It was
Beata of Salamanca. She was accused of having made a pact with the
emissary of hell, whose plague breath passes through everyone. As late as
1820, 21 prisoners were found in the Inquisition dungeons of Madrid,
some of whom had been waiting for their execution for years. Not one of
them knew the name of the city, none knew exactly what he was accused
of. One of the freed prisoners was to be executed the next day." (Bergmeier, R. 2018)

13.3.c Censorship

Censorship by the church also increasingly lost its power. With the transformation of Christianity into state-church narcissism from the 4th century onwards, the pathological was declared normal and passed on culturally for centuries. Alternatives were suppressed by means of censorship.

The dissolution of the authority of the church and rulers in the 19th century led to a reduction in censorship, but the pathological, which had been defined as normal for centuries, remained deeply rooted in society - to this day.

On the one hand, the Catholic Church did not issue the dogma of the infallibility of the Pope in his function as God's representative until 1870, which had not been necessary in the centuries before.

On the other hand, no longer prevented by strict censorship, a multitude of new faiths and salvation ideologies emerged.

And so today we have a bouquet of irrational, quasi-religious forms of expression that complement or replace the dogmas and promises of salvation of Catholicism:

• Steiner's (1861-1925) anthroposophy: with kindergartens, schools, facilities for people with disabilities...

In the field of medicine,

• alternative practitioners

emerge, with treatment methods that are far removed from science, such as

• Hahnemann's (1755-1843) globules
• Schüssler's (1821-1898) salts
• Bach's (1886-1936) flowers

In the relatively young field of psychology, among others,

• Freud's (1856-1939) psychoanalysis

and

• Watson's (1878-1958) behaviorism

emerge as a result of the democratization of the dogmatically irrational, and as an ideological replacement for the exclusive promise of salvation of Catholicism.

"Und in so viele Sekten, Meinungen und Pfaffenschaften sie auch auseinanderfallen, sie beten alle das eine Gebet, welches schon Kolumbus betete, als er dies Land betrat: 'Gott, lasse mich in Deiner Barmherzigkeit die große Goldmine finden.'" (Lessing, Th. 1929/2021)[61]

13.4   Freud

Freud is the mythomaniac realization of the dogma of the solipsistic, self-developing ego, which has been consolidated by Catholicism for centuries. It is Freud's myths that continue to shape Western[62] psychology and psychotherapy, their framework of meaning, to a large extent, and stand in the way of a scientifically based psychology.

"Freud hatte erklärt, dass das Unbewusste im Erwachsenen »von dem schlummernden Kinde in ihm geprägt würde, dem Kind, das von einem besseren Leben so intensiv träumt und im Wachzustand fantasiert, dass der Erwachsene manchmal Realität und Fantasie nicht unterscheiden kann«. Und das Kind könne es auch nicht, behauptete Freud. Mit anderen Worten: Ein Kind könne maßgeblich von seinem Fantasieleben beeinflusst sein und nicht von realen Ereignissen. Dies würde bedeuten,

---

61   "And no matter how many sects, opinions and clergy they fall into, they all pray the one prayer that Columbus prayed when he set foot on this land: 'God, let me find the great gold mine in your mercy.'" (Lessing, Th. 1929/2021)

62   For a good overview of Russian psychology, which has largely rejected and still rejects Freud's "theories", see e.g. Bassin, F. V. (1978)

dass das, was Eltern mit dem Kind anstellen, nicht annähernd so bedeutungsvoll sei wie die inneren Vorstellungen, Wünsche und Fantasien des Kindes über den Elternteil. Die Berührung der Mutter könnte zum Beispiel als liebevolle Zuwendung gemeint sein, aber in einen sexuellen Traum des Kindes umgewandelt werden. Wenn ein Kind über sexuellen Missbrauch berichtet, kann das lediglich die Offenbarung eines Wunsches sein. Vielleicht war die Erinnerung an eine Verführung in Wirklichkeit die Erinnerung an einen Wunsch, ein sexueller Traum, der zu gleichen Teilen aus Imagination und Sehnsucht »gewebt« war. Kleine Kinder besäßen einen mächtigen erotischen Drang, der bewirke, dass sie ihren gegengeschlechtlichen Elternteil sexuell begehren, meinte Freud. Die Realität müsse damit überhaupt nichts zu tun haben." (Blum, D. 2010)[63]

So if a child is mistreated and/or sexually abused by parents and/or relatives, then this is either just a fantasy of the child, or if it is true, then it is not the fault of the adults, but of the child and his strong erotic urge[64].

---

63 "Freud had explained that the unconscious in the adult is "shaped by the slumbering child within him, the child who dreams of a better life and fantasizes so intensely in his waking state that the adult sometimes cannot distinguish reality from fantasy." And neither can the child, Freud claimed. In other words, a child can be significantly influenced by his fantasy life rather than by real events. This would mean that what parents do with the child is not nearly as meaningful as the child's inner ideas, wishes and fantasies about the parent. The mother's touch, for example, might be intended as loving attention but be transformed into a sexual dream for the child. When a child reports sexual abuse, it may simply be the revelation of a wish. Perhaps the memory of a seduction was actually the memory of a wish, a sexual dream "woven" of equal parts imagination and longing. Freud believed that small children have a powerful erotic urge that causes them to sexually desire their opposite-sex parent. Reality does not necessarily have anything to do with this." (Blum, D. 2010)

64 See: Schmidt, B. (2017): Autismus und der Kühlschrankmutter Mythos.

And it is Freud who has shaped our "understanding" of narcissism so far, and thereby ultimately prevented it.[65]

"Sigmund Freud first developed narcissism as a central psychoanalytic concept in his 1914 essay 'On Narcissism: An Introduction'. In this essay, Freud states that he has discovered that a primary narcissism is necessary for the ego, to be 'born'. Previously, Freud had thought the mother the first love object of all subjects, but in this essay narcissism supplants this primary mother-love and is used to describe a process in which we become subjects by taking our 'self' as our first love object. Freud differentiates between primary narcissism, the process that inaugurates subjectivity, and secondary forms of narcissism, which he suggests can be normal or pathological depending on its degree.

Freud suggests that primary narcissism, the birth of a conscious self whom we identify with and direct our love towards, is inaugurated by the incorporation of an 'ego-ideal' that is instilled in the infant via the voice and gaze of the parents and 'the common ideal of a family, a class or a nation' (1991: 96). For the individual subject this ideal is imagined as possessing 'every perfection which is of value' (1991: 88) and becomes 'the substitute for the lost narcissism of […] childhood' (1991: 94). Freud argues that the (inevitable) non-fulfilment of this ideal is experienced by the child as a fear of punishment – the fear of losing the parent's love. As we grow up, our ego-ideal is continually adapted by 'public opinion', and failure to approximate it is experienced as guilt and social anxiety (1991: 97). The ego-ideal is tyrannical, it 'constantly watches the actual ego and measures it by that ideal' (1991: 89). Freud is insistent on this point: 'A power of this kind, watching, discovering and cri-

---

65   Eine frühe, umfassende und fundierte Kritik an Freuds Mythen findet sich bei Bühler, Karl (1927): Die Krise der Psychologie

ticizing all our intentions, does really exist. It exists in every one of us in normal life' (1991: 90)." (Tyler, I. 2007)

When Karl Kraus says that psychoanalysis is the disease it claims to cure, he is probably right.

From the perspective presented here, Freud shows four elements of the symptom complex of the narcissistic personality:

1. Pronounced addiction problems
2. Mythomania
3. Denial of reality
4. Lack of awareness of wrongdoing (analysis of his daughter) of which at least the last three can also be found in Watson, and following him in Skinner.

13.5   Watson

"Nicht nur, dass der watsonsche Behaviorismus und das pawlowsche Konditionieren[66] dominant waren. Wissenschaftler hatten seit Jahrhunderten behauptet, dass Tiere im Grunde dumm sind. Die anderen Spezies konnten zwar konditioniert werden, man konnte sie zu einer Reaktion veranlassen; aber denken, fühlen, analysieren, trauern – niemals. Im 17. Jahrhundert verglich der französische Philosoph Rene Descartes Tiere mit Maschinen, Tiere könnten niemals wie Menschen denken, meinte er. Sie seien seelenlose Kreaturen, Maschinenungeheuer. Diese Vorstellung hielt sogar an, als Charles Darwin seine evolutionären Argumente anführte. Charles Darwin behauptete unbestreitbar, dass Menschen und andere Spezies gemeinsame Hirnstrukturen und demzufolge auch gemeinsame Fähigkeiten haben mussten. Das war für Goldstein zu viel, er reagierte kategorisch mit Ablehnung. Aber selbst jene, die an Darwin glaubten,

---

66   The theory of I. P. Pavlov is much more sophisticated than it is perceived in the West. See Pavlov, I. P. "Psychopathology and Psychiatry"

konnten nicht gänzlich akzeptieren, dass Tiere die Art eines komplexen Hirns besaßen, das lange Zeit ausschließlich Menschen vorbehalten war." (Blum, D. 2010)[67]

This view must be corrected insofar as there were and are scientists who saw and see a direct connection between the development of humans and animals, including in the area of intelligence and consciousness. Such as John G. Romanes (1885/2021) and Lloyd C. Morgan (1894) as founders of ethology, up to its modern representatives such as Konrad Lorenz, Nico Tinbergen and Irenäus Eibl-Eibesfeldt (2004), to name just a few.
It is the dogmatic separation into body and mind, into humanities and natural sciences, that has so far stood in the way of enlightenment here. It is therefore always revealing that in the bibliographies of authors who deal with the relationship between consciousness, mind and brain, such as Gerald Edelman (2005), only philosophers and no ethologists can be found.

Watson replaces the pseudo-empathy of Catholicism with an anti-empathy, but like the torturers in the dungeons of the Inquisition, with the aim of saving poor (children's) souls.

---

67 "Not only were Watsonian behaviorism and Pavlovian conditioning dominant. Scientists had claimed for centuries that animals were basically stupid. Other species could be conditioned, they could be made to react, but they could never think, feel, analyze, mourn. In the 17th century, the French philosopher Rene Descartes compared animals to machines, saying that animals could never think like humans. They were soulless creatures, machine monsters. This idea persisted even when Charles Darwin made his evolutionary arguments. Charles Darwin indisputably claimed that humans and other species must have common brain structures and therefore common abilities. This was too much for Goldstein, who reacted categorically with rejection. But even those who believed in Darwin could not fully accept that animals had the kind of complex brain that had long been exclusive to humans." (Blum, D. 2010)

"An Watson wird heute oft als an einen Wissenschaftler erinnert, der einen professionellen Kreuzzug gegen die Übel der Liebe und Zuneigung führte.»Wenn man versucht ist, sein Kind zu liebkosen, erinnere man sich, dass Mutterliebe ein gefährliches Instrument ist«, warnte Watson. Zu häufiges Liebkosen und Hätscheln könnten die frühe Kindheit unglücklich und die Jugend zu einem Albtraum machen, das Kind sogar so sehr verziehen, dass es später heiratsuntauglich wird. Und das, warnte Watson, kann in einer unerhört kurzen Zeit geschehen: »Wenn der Charakter eines Kindes erst einmal durch schlechte Behandlung ruiniert worden ist, was schon innerhalb weniger Tage passieren kann, wer könnte dann wissen, ob der Schaden jemals reparabel ist?«" (Blum, D. 2010)[68]

From the beginning, behaviorism was subject to extensive criticism from many sides, including from Arthur Koestler.

„Früher neigten die Naturforscher zum Anthropomorphismus, das heißt, sie schrieben den Tieren menschenähnliche Verstandeskräfte und Empfindungen zu. 1894 postulierte Lloyd Morgan ein Prinzip, das zu einer Art elften Gebots für Psychologen und als »Lloyd-Morgan-Regel« bekannt wurde. Sie besagt, daß man zur Deutung der Reaktionen eines Tieres nicht auf geistige Prozesse des Menschen zurückgreifen dürfe, wenn sich die Reaktion durch einfachere Prozesse auf niederer Stufe erklären

---

68   "Watson is often remembered today as a scientist who led a professional crusade against the evils of love and affection.»When you are tempted to caress your child, remember that motherly love is a dangerous instrument,« Watson warned. Too much caressing and coddling could make early childhood miserable, adolescence a nightmare, and even spoil the child so much that it becomes unfit for marriage later on. And this, Watson warned, can happen in an incredibly short time: »Once a child's character has been ruined by bad treatment, which can happen in a matter of days, who can know whether the damage can ever be repaired?«" (Blum, D. 2010)

lasse. Die Verhaltenswissenschaft hat dieses Prinzip auf den Kopf gestellt. Sie lehnt es ab, dem Menschen geistige Prozesse zuzuerkennen, die nicht auch bei niederen Tieren nachgewiesen werden können.

Mit andern Worten: Die Behavioristen haben das anthropomorphistische Rattenbild durch das rattomorphistische Menschenbild ersetzt." (Koestler, A. 1980)[69]

However, Koestler is also a victim of the division between the humanities and natural sciences, and has almost certainly not read Lloyd C. Morgan (1894) or his predecessor George J. Romanes (1885/2021).

And the title of Arthur Koestler's book (1980) also makes one sit up and take notice:

"The Poverty of Psychology. Man as a Victim of the Attempt to Deal with Irrational Behavior with Rational Methods."

How else should one try to deal with irrational behavior than with rational methods?

With a rational method that, above all, must repeatedly question one's own foundations of thought, as already mentioned at the beginning - as happened here.

69　"In the past, natural scientists tended towards anthropomorphism, that is, they attributed human-like intellectual powers and feelings to animals. In 1894, Lloyd Morgan postulated a principle that became a kind of eleventh commandment for psychologists and became known as the "Lloyd Morgan Rule". It states that one should not resort to human mental processes to interpret the reactions of an animal if the reaction can be explained by simpler, lower-level processes. Behavioral science has turned this principle on its head. It refuses to attribute mental processes to humans that cannot also be demonstrated in lower animals.

In other words: the behaviorists have replaced the anthropomorphic image of the rat with the rattomorphic image of man." (Koestler, A. 1980)

The whole supposed problem arose from the dogmas of Catholicism, and made Watson's madness possible in the first place, which is still deeply rooted in society today. And consequently, the problem can only be solved by overcoming the dogmas of Catholicism.

"Watsons Psychologie stand in nahezu vollständigem Gegensatz zu der beziehungsorientierten Theorie, die Harlow später entwickelte. Stattdessen argumentierte Watson, dass die Erwachsenen – Eltern, Lehrer und Ärzte – Kinder verstärkt konditionieren und erziehen sollten. Ihre Aufgabe sei es, die richtigen Reize zu liefern und die korrekte Reaktion herbeizuführen. Und genau das war es, was Watson 1928 überzeugend in seinem Bestseller zur psychologischen Betreuung des Kindes und Säuglings *The Psychological Care of the Child and Infant* erörterte. Der britische Philosoph Bertrand Russell erklärte das Buch zum ersten Erziehungsratgeber von wissenschaftlichem Wert. Watson, sagte er, hatte beim Studium der Babys in der Weise Erfolg wie »ein Wissenschaftler, der die Amöbe studiert«. Der Atlantic Monthly nannte den Bestseller unentbehrlich, in der New York Times hieß es, dass mit Watsons Veröffentlichung »eine neue Epoche in der Geistesgeschichte der Menschheit« begonnen habe. Die Zeitschrift Parents hielt seine Ratschläge für einen unentbehrlichen Pflichttitel im Bücherregal aller aufgeklärten Eltern." (Blum, D. 2010)[70]

---

[70] "Watson's psychology was almost completely at odds with the relationship-oriented theory that Harlow later developed. Instead, Watson argued that adults - parents, teachers and doctors - should be more involved in conditioning and educating children. Their job was to provide the right stimuli and bring about the correct response.
And that is exactly what Watson convincingly discussed in his 1928 bestseller on the psychological care of children and infants, The Psychological Care of the Child and Infant. The British philosopher Bertrand Russell declared the book to be the first parenting guide of scientific value. Watson, he said, succeeded in studying babies in the way that "a scientist stu-

While philosophers for centuries fled from reality into their metaphysical ivory towers and the "phenomenology of the mind", thereby ignoring the madness and life with its dangers as well as its beauties, modern "scientists" of psychology flee into their laboratories. Laboratories are designed to be alien to the world, so that experiments can be carried out in a controlled manner, unaffected by the whims of the world. That is the purpose of laboratories. But if you lock yourself in the laboratory, deny the world outside the laboratory, and do not repeatedly establish the relationship between the laboratory and the world, then that is escapism. From the narcissistic symptom complex, Watson exhibits:

1. Dogmatism – ignoring a large part of reality

2. Ideology – as an exclusive promise of salvation

3. Missionary work – everything and everyone had to be conditioned using behaviorism

4. Intolerance

Watson thus exhibits a far-reaching megalomania that suppresses reality and vitality, which goes far beyond the results of the conditioning experiments and leads to utopian fantasies:

"Watson schrieb, dass er von einer Babyfarm träume, wo Hunderte von Säuglingen ihren Eltern weggenommen werden könnten, um dann nach wissenschaftlichen Prinzipien aufgezo-

---

dies the amoeba." The Atlantic Monthly called the bestseller indispensable, and the New York Times said that Watson's publication had begun "a new era in the intellectual history of mankind." Parents magazine considered his advice an indispensable must-have on the bookshelf of every enlightened parent." (Blum, D. 2010)

gen zu werden. Ideal wäre es, wenn eine Mutter nicht einmal wisse, welches Kind ihr eigenes sei, und es demzufolge nicht verderben könne. Emotionale Reaktionen auf Kinder sollten mithilfe eines aufklärenden wissenschaftlichen Verfahrens kontrolliert werden, empfahl Watson. Eltern sollten aktiv mitwirken, ihre Kinder mithilfe von einfachen, objektiven Konditionierungstechniken zu prägen." (Blum, D. 2010)[71]

13.6   Jewish Psychology

In politics, the beginning of the 20th century was the time of dictatorships and dictators, such as
• Hitler (1889-1945),
• Mussolini (1883-1945),
• Stalin (1878-1953) ...

This had dramatic consequences for the development of psychology.

Up until the 1930s there was a very lively and diverse psychology, whose key figures were often Jews. After what has been said so far, it is hardly surprising that it was Jewish psychologists who represented a comprehensive and, above all, social-psychological approach. And this in the West and the East, and in lively exchange with one another. It was therefore mainly Jewish psychologists who played a key role in the constructive development of the young discipline of psychology. To name

---

[71]   "Watson wrote that he dreamed of a baby farm where hundreds of infants could be taken from their parents and then raised according to scientific principles. Ideally, a mother would not even know which child was her own and thus could not spoil it. Emotional reactions to children should be controlled using an enlightening scientific process, Watson recommended. Parents should actively participate in shaping their children using simple, objective conditioning techniques." (Blum, D. 2010)

their names here would go beyond the scope, so great was their number.

This development was destroyed by both the totalitarian regimes and the Second World War, and above all by the persecution, expulsion and murder of the Jews... by National Socialism.

The torture chambers of the Inquisition were replaced by the torture chambers of the totalitarian regimes.

Instead of being burned at the stake, people now died by murder or in concentration camps.

For example, Theodor Lessing, who is often quoted here, was shot by Nazi henchmen in 1933 in his exile in Marienbad. It can be assumed that this was not just to the delight of the Nazis, given his extensive and sharp criticism.

In the Soviet Union, the works of Lev S. Vygotsky were viewed critically as early as 1934 and were completely banned from 1936.

"Vygotsky and his theory of cultural-historical psychology were also subjected to sharp attacks and political-ideological polemics, which were also directed against his students and colleagues. These accusations essentially related to the theory's lack of a class standpoint - which is certainly true - and to his understanding of Marxism, which was in fact incompatible with economistic or vulgar Marxism, as well as to his relationships - personal or literary - with politicians (such as Trotsky), philosophers (such as Deborin), economists (such as Bukharin), psychologists (such as Blonsky) or writers (such as Mande'stam or Gumil'ev) who have since been officially condemned. (See Van der Veer/Valsiner 1991, p. 360ff.) The fact that Vygotsky drew on so extensively from »Western« literature and its »idealistic« concepts – such as Freud's psychoanalysis, Watson's behaviorism, Köhler's Gestalt theory, Stern's personalism and Bühler's theory of language – and was even able to extract positive aspects from the »bourgeois« theories of the »class enemy«, as his numerous translations, introductions and reviews – Freud (1925), Koffka (1926, 1934), Thorndike (1926), Ruble (1926), Hall (1927), Köhler (1929, 1930), Clara and William Stern (1929), K. Bühler (1929), Bühler/Hetzer/Tudor (1930), Gesell (1932) and Piaget (1932) – prove. ...

The situation changed suddenly and completely with the infamous paedology decree of July 3, 1936, in which the CPSU intervened at the highest level in the ideological "battle for the 3rd front" - in official parlance, this was the "scientific front" alongside the "war front" and the "production front". With a stroke of the pen, the decree liquidated an entire extensive and urgently needed social practice - all establishments, institutions, organizations, journals and leading scientists of the entire paedological movement - ultimately because, in Stalin's opinion, they were capable of impairing the party's monopoly on definition. From then on, there were not even any more disputes. Vygotsky's name disappeared from literature for two decades. His books were destroyed and his name was deleted from the editors' lists of journals, congress reports and anthologies. But opportunities arise where, beyond these connections, a new translation based on the current state of knowledge can make Vygotsky's roots in the pan-European psychological tradition visible and at the same time make it clear that Vygotsky's cultural-historical theory was not an isolated special development in the Soviet Union, but a specific further development of the psychological theories favored and discussed in Europe as a whole. One could even formulate the thesis that the date 1936 affected European psychology as a whole because it ended the communication that had been so productive up to that point and thereby hindered the development not only of Russian but also of Western European psychology." (Preface in: Vygotskij, L. 2017)

After the end of World War II and the Nazi regime, the constructive past was denied in psychology in the West instead of reconnecting with it. The past can only be denied and repressed in its entirety. Differentiating between good and bad, constructive and destructive, would require precisely the confrontation with the past that one wants to avoid.
The Jewish psychologists were either dead or in exile.
The previously pan-European psychology with intensive exchange was divided into East and West. In the West, people adopted American-style psychological primitivism on a large scale, including in the form of behaviorism, instead of coming to terms with their own past, for better or for worse.
Jaan Valsiner and Aaro Toomela repeatedly and quite rightly emphasize that pre-war psychology needs to be considered in order to counter the errors of mainstream psychology and the pseudo-empiricism that goes with it. But the reasons for ignoring pre-war psychology have remained hidden to them so far.

As a society as a whole, people were highly traumatized by the war, which had no longer just taken place on a distant front. In Germany, people plunged into a consumer frenzy as compensation and a form of narcissistic escape.
The decades of the economic miracle came.

13.7   Narcissism is something you have to be able to afford

The ignoring of reality, the creation of one's own, albeit small, empire, which are characteristic of the narcissistic personality disorder, i.e. the "unreality" described by Lowen, requires corresponding degrees of freedom and corresponding resources. Most people up to the 19th century had neither the degrees of freedom nor the necessary resources that make ignoring reality possible. Mistakes were reported back as such and often led to death. Only an economy of abundance and the resulting freedoms enable the emergence of narcissistic personality disorders in large numbers - and not only in the 20th century.

On an individual level, an affluent society offers enough stable "ecological niches" in which narcissists can compensate. In these niches, narcissists appear inconspicuous. This changes when the security of the niches and the associated pseudo-reality constructs are threatened or disrupted, as we are currently experiencing due to the corona virus.

Our age, the cultural basis of our society, is neither crazy, as Lowen (1992) considers, nor is it particularly narcissistic. It simply offers the freedom and independence, a decontextualized life and thus "unreality", which enables a numerous occurrence of narcissistic personality disorders, as a disease of civilization, so to speak.

"Meine These besagt, daß Narzißmus im Einzelmenschen und in der Kultur einen gewissen Grad von Unwirklichkeit anzeigt. Unwirklichkeit ist nicht einfach nur neurotisch, sie grenzt ans Psychotische. An einem Verhaltensmuster, das das Erringen von Erfolgen über das Bedürfnis stellt, zu lieben und geliebt zu werden, ist etwas Verrücktes. Ein Mensch, der keinen Kontakt zur Realität seines Wesens – zum Körper und seinen Gefühlen hat, ist etwas verrückt. Und eine Kultur, die Luft, Wasser und Erde im Namen eines »höheren« Lebensstandards verschmutzt und verseucht, hat etwas Verrücktes an sich."
(Lowen, A. 1992)[72]

---

72   "My thesis is that narcissism in the individual and in the culture indicates
     a certain degree of unreality. Unreality is not just neurotic, it borders on

But unreality occurs in two different forms. On the one hand, it is the unreality/decontextualization required by a culture as a prerequisite for the development of narcissistic personality disorders – and it is also a symptom of narcissists.

„Aber kann eine Kultur geisteskrank sein? Diese Vorstellung ist in der Psychiatrie keineswegs selbstverständlich. Im allgemeinen sieht man Geisteskrankheit als Kennzeichen eines Individuums an, das den Kontakt zur Realität seiner Kultur verloren hat. Nach diesem Kriterium (das seine Gültigkeit hat) ist der erfolgreiche narzißtische Mensch weit davon entfernt, geisteskrank zu sein. Es sei denn ... es sei denn, natürlich, daß der Kultur eine gewisse Geisteskrankheit innewohnt."
(Lowen, A. 1992)[73]

Lowen is wrong on several counts here.
Firstly, there are no successful narcissists, at least not in the long term. Narcissism always has an (auto-)destructive effect (Schmidt, B.; Ganz, A. 2017).
Secondly, as already mentioned, a culture cannot be narcissistic; it can only encourage the development of narcissistic personality disorders and at the same time offer narcissists a great deal of freedom, including freedom to compensate for the per-

---

the psychotic. There is something crazy about a behavior pattern that puts the achievement of success above the need to love and be loved. A person who is out of touch with the reality of his being - his body and his feelings - is a little crazy. And there is something crazy about a culture that pollutes and contaminates air, water and earth in the name of a "higher" standard of living." (Lowen, A. 1992)

73 "But can a culture be insane? This idea is by no means self-evident in psychiatry. In general, insanity is seen as a sign of an individual who has lost touch with the reality of his culture. According to this criterion (which is valid), the successful narcissistic person is far from being insane. Unless... unless, of course, there is a certain insanity inherent in the culture." (Lowen, A. 1992)

sonality disorder. The psychological disorder, i.e. the lack of adaptation to reality, only becomes apparent when it becomes apparent that necessary compensation mechanisms are missing or fail due to external changes, such as collectively in the case of a corona pandemic.

13.8   Increasing Degrees of Freedom II

Thus, the economic developments after the end of World War II naturally offer further degrees of freedom, which build on those from the changes of the 19th century already described.

"The saga of the Me Decade begins with one of those facts that is so big and so obvious (like the Big Dipper), no one ever comments on it anymore. Namely: the 30-year boom. Wartime spending in the United States in the 1940s touched off a boom that has continued for more than 30 years. It has pumped money into every class level of the population on a scale without parallel in any country in history." (Wolfe , T. 1976)

Many people, and no longer just clergy and rulers, suddenly have the ability to ignore reality. But not all people have these degrees of freedom, nor do all people with the necessary degrees of freedom develop a narcissistic personality disorder. The degrees of freedom, i.e. the separation from the direct feedback of reality, are only necessary, but not sufficient.

At the same time, the degrees of freedom of the affluent economy also offer the opportunity to join together in appropriate groups. The democratization of the irrational can thus be lived out not only individually, but also collectively in substitute religions (see also Schmidt, B.; Ganz, A. 2017).

"The encounter session—although it was not called that—was also a staple practice in psychedelic communes and, for that matter, in New Left communes. In fact, the analysis of the self, and of one another, was unceasing. But in these groups and at Esalen and in movements such as Arica there were two common assumptions that distinguished them from the aristocratic lemon sessions and personality finishings of yore. The first was: I, with the help of my brothers and sisters, must strip away all the shams and excess baggage of society and my upbringing in order to find the Real Me. Scientology uses the word "clear" to identify the state that one must strive for. But just what is that state? And what will the Real Me be like? It is at this point that the new movements tend to take on a religious or spiritual atmosphere. In one form or another they arrive at an axiom first propounded by the Gnostic Christians some 1,800 years ago: namely, that at the apex of every human soul there exists a spark of the light of God. In most mortals that spark is "asleep" (the Gnostics' word), all but smothered by the facades and general falseness of society. But those souls who are clear can find that spark within themselves and unite their souls with God's. And with that conviction comes the second assumption: There is an other order that actually reigns supreme in the world. Like the light of God itself, this other order is invisible to most mortals. But he who has dug himself out from under the junk heap of civilization can discover it." (Wolfe, T. 1976)

The narcissism of kings, popes and cardinals, the self-proclaimed representatives of God and rulers by the grace of God, is now affecting many people.

"The various movements of the current religious wave ... begin with . . . "Let's talk about Me." They begin with the most delicious look inward; with considerable narcissism, in short.

When the believers bind together into religions, it is always with a sense of splitting off from the rest of society. We, the enlightened (lit by the sparks at the apexes of our souls), hereby separate ourselves from the lost souls around us. Like all religions before them, they proselytize—but always on promising the opposite of nationalism: a City of Light that is above it all." (Wolfe, T. 1976)

However, it is difficult to determine how large this proportion of the total population really is. A major problem is that dogmatic, ideological and intolerant positions are always easier and more offensive to represent in public and always lead to proselytizing than differentiated, self-critical ones. We are currently experiencing a massive dominance of narcissistic positions in public discourse, which by no means means that these positions also predominate in the population.

13.8.a   Digitalization and "social" media

If one does not perceive the dynamics of development, from the infection with the narcissism virus in 380 by the Cunctos Populos, through a long incubation period to the present day, then the current culture naturally appears to be the root of all evil.

"In The Global Village (1992), Marshall McLuhan and Bruce Powers warned that narcissism was 'the fastest developing social disease of the peoples of the West' (1992: 100). The claim that consumer-orientated and media-saturated cultures have given rise to an 'immense narcissism' has been repeatedly asserted within social and cultural criticism for the past 40 years. Within cultural studies there has been a recent proliferation of accounts of narcissism in analyses of consumer culture, celebrity culture and new media. For example, P. David Marshall cites a rise in narcissism as the reason for the growth in popularity of 'reality' genres, arguing that 'a new era of public narcissism is mutating with new media forms' (2004). And influential media theorist Lev Manovich claims that most new media activate a 'narcissistic condition' (2001: 235). It is against the backdrop of this resurgence of interest in narcissism as a descriptive term and conceptual device within cultural studies that this article sets out to explore the history of claims that narcissism is the pathology of our time." (Tyler, I. 2007)

It is the degrees of freedom created by a prosperous society, the independence from the often unfriendly reality, the cultural "unreality", which of course also affects communication. It is no longer the farmers who talk about the expected weather on which the success of their harvest and thus, in case of doubt, their survival depends. Information becomes arbitrary, becomes unreal[74]. This is certainly not only good, but it is also a necessary consequence of our independence. If you read about the lives of famous people from the 19th century, for example Mark Twain, you will also read about a very high (child) mortality rate, which we have overcome today.

"Doch der größte Teil der täglichen Nachrichten bleibt wirkungslos, besteht aus Informationen, über die wir reden können, die uns jedoch nicht zu sinnvollem Handeln veranlassen. Dies ist das wichtigste Vermächtnis des Telegraphen: Dadurch, daß er eine Fülle irrelevanter Informationen hervorbrachte, hat er das proportionale Verhältnis zwischen Information und Aktion drastisch verändert.

Es ist in diesem Zusammenhang aufschlußreich, daß sich das Kreuzworträtsel in Amerika genau um die Zeit zu einem popu-

---

74   siehe hierzu z.B.: Postman, Neil (1988): Wir amüsieren uns zu Tode.

lären Zeitvertreib entwickelte, als der Telegraph und die Photo-
graphie die Nachrichten verwandelt und aus funktionalen Informationen dekontextualisierte Fakten gemacht hatten. Dieses
zeitliche Zusammentreffen deutet darauf hin, daß die neuen
Technologien das jahrhundertealte Problem der Information auf
den Kopf gestellt hatten: Während die Menschen früher nach
Informationen suchten, um den realen Kontext ihres Daseins zu
erhellen, mußten sie jetzt Kontexte erfinden, in denen sich
sonst nutzlose Informationen scheinbar nutzbringend gebrau-
chen ließen. Das Kreuzworträtsel ist ein derartiger Pseudo-
Kontext; die Cocktail Party ist ein anderer; wieder andere sind
die Radioquizsendungen der dreißiger und vierziger Jahre und
die heutigen Ratespiele im Fernsehen; den Extrempunkt mar-
kiert wohl das erfolgreiche Spiel »Trivial Pursuit«. Auf diese
oder jene Weise beantworten sie alle die Frage: »Was soll ich
mit all diesen zusammenhanglosen Fakten anfangen?« Und im
Grunde genommen ist die Antwort immer die gleiche: Warum
benutzt du sie nicht zur Zerstreuung? Zur Unterhaltung? Um
dich damit zu amüsieren? In einem Spiel?" (Postman, N.
1988)[75]

---

75 "But most of the daily news remains ineffective, consisting of information
we can talk about but which does not lead us to meaningful action. This is
the most important legacy of the telegraph: by generating a wealth of irrelevant information, it drastically changed the proportional relationship
between information and action.
It is telling in this connection that the crossword puzzle became a popular
pastime in America precisely at the time when the telegraph and photo-
graphy had transformed the news, turning functional information into decontextualized facts. This coincidence suggests that the new technologies
had turned the centuries-old problem of information on its head: whereas
previously people had sought information to illuminate the real context of
their existence, they now had to invent contexts in which otherwise use-
less information could apparently be put to useful use. The crossword
puzzle is one such pseudo-context; the cocktail party is another; others are
the radio quiz shows of the 1930s and 1940s and today's television quiz-
zes; the extreme point is probably the successful game "Trivial Pursuit".

Culture does not follow the Catholic dogma of either good or evil. Culture often leads to a detachment from nature, from a liberation from the constraints and threats associated with it. And, at least according to Theodor Lessing, through this process it leads to the "destruction of the earth through spirit" (Lessing, Th. 1929/2021).
The degrees of freedom achieved through culture and above all technology are of course also degrees of freedom for narcissists.

"A grandiose yet vulnerable self-concept appears to underlie the chronic goal of obtaining continuous external self-affirmation. Because narcissists are insensitive to others' concerns and social constraints and view others as inferior, their self-regulatory efforts often are counterproductive and ultimately prevent the positive feedback that they seek—thus undermining the self they are trying to create and maintain."
(Morf; Rhodewaldt 2001)

When Morf and Rhodewaldt wrote this, the supposedly "social" media had not yet been invented. But these media now offer the possibility of joining together in mutually affirming groups, far removed from any reality. "Communities of ignorance" are formed, which only exist in their self-created bubbles, affirming each other.
But that is only one side of the coin.
Without these degrees of freedom, for example, writing this book would be impossible.

In one way or another, they all answer the question: "What am I supposed to do with all these unrelated facts?" And basically the answer is always the same: Why don't you use them for diversion? For entertainment? To amuse yourself with them? In a game?" (Postman, N. 1988)

INDIVIDUALLY

Current Western psychology is WEIRD, and that in two ways. Firstly, as an abbreviation:

„It has been widely acknowledged today that the vast majority of participants in psychology studies (97% to be exact) come from the "Western World" (67% from the USA), which are WEIRD (Western educated industrialized, rich, and democratic) outliers within the span of humanity (Henrich, Heine, and Norenzayan, 2010).[76]" (Wagoner; Christensen; Demuth 2021)

One should keep in mind that Freud's dogmas could not have originated in another culture, and indeed must have seemed downright absurd there before they were established as "science", such as in Russia (see Bassin, F. V. 1978).

On the other hand, however, as a word - with "strange" in the mildest form.
So current mainstream psychology is based on the (Catholic) dogmas presented in the cultural-historical part.
What was still a crisis of diversity for Karl Bühler (1927) became a crisis of divisions into dogmas and a psychological primitivism largely adopted from the USA due to the National Socialists and the Second World War.
The question raised by Zittoun et al. (2009) as to whether the current crisis in psychology is not actually more a matter of differentiation than a crisis due to fragmentation must be answered in the negative. The essential difference between fragmentation and differentiation is that in the latter, in addition to ana-

---

76   It should be noted that these characteristics, with the exception of "western", have only emerged in the last two hundred (industrialized) or one hundred (educated, rich, democratic) years.

lysis, synthesis is not only possible, but is also implemented again and again. Like a watchmaker who puts the watch he is repairing back together to check its function.

However, current Western psychology is not only fragmented into random areas, but is largely based on dogmas such as Freudian psychoanalysis. And it lacks the ability to mytholysis, i.e. to dissolve the fundamental myths and dogmas, which is an essential basis for a science.

The young discipline of psychology is therefore in a situation comparable to astrology before Copernicus and the turning point named after him.

In summary, it can be said that our society offers optimal conditions for narcissistic personality disorders in the form of great degrees of freedom and compensation options, but is not itself sick or narcissistic.

And secondly, one should not assume that there is a high proportion of narcissists in the population just because they are often overrepresented in public discourse with their dogmatic, intolerant and missionary positions[77].

At the same time, however, it should also be clear that our understanding of narcissism as a disease has at least been influenced, if not prevented, by the dogmas of Catholicism that have shaped people's self-image for centuries.

---

77 Examples in Germany include gender discussions, renaming of supposed-ly racist names such as "Mohren Apotheke", the supposed problem of "cultural appropriation" and other forms of Western manifestations of a "Sharia police". Always based on the narcissistic feeling of moral superiority, dogmatic intolerance and the compulsive need to bully and harass other people. The list can be supplemented by vegans and (militant) climate and animal protectors. See e.g. Schmidt, B.; Ganz, A. (2017), and Schmidt, B. (2022). But also by the so-called „Reichsbürger", who claim "L'État, c'est moi!".

14   „I am the ding[78]"

I owe a large part of the insights written down here to a boy of about four who, on a warm summer day, was hopping from one foot to the other, wearing only rubber boots and underpants. While doing this, he sang with a slight speech impediment, in the presence of other children, and in answer to the question of what they should play together:

"I am the ding, I am the ding. And you must do what I say." Hardly anything gets to the heart of narcissism better than this image. The narcissist's core statement is "I am the ding!", in underpants and rubber boots.

The problem with the boy was not that he wanted to be ding SOMETIMES, but that he actually ALWAYS wanted to play THIS game - ALWAYS with HIM as ding.

And that he was neither aware of his speech impediment nor of his somewhat silly outfit, similar to the fairy tale emperor's new clothes. Here we can already see the difference between the desired self-portrayal and the self-revelation that is actually realized. A self-proclaimed "ruler by the grace of God" in miniature format.

In his self-created kingdom, in which he always decides everything as king, and so supposedly has everything under control and therefore believes himself to be safe.

And, since the king decides everything, including the rules, and is both a legislator and a judge, the king can never do wrong. At the same time, there can and must be no one higher than the king, but also no one on the same level.

And any criticism of the king is seen as an insult to the king's majesty and is mercilessly pursued.

---

78   Since he couldn't pronounce the "k" and spoke a "d" instead, the "King" became a "Ding". In German it is "Dönig" instead of "König".

15 Ontogenesis

In mainstream clinical psychology, which is based on Freud's mythomaniac speculations, it seems unnecessary for pathology to see ontogenesis as the basis for pathogenesis. However, it is necessary to consider the areas of ontogenesis that serve to understand the pathogenesis of narcissism. This is the only way to grasp and understand the variety of possible paths to the development of a narcissistic personality disorder.

The pathogenesis of narcissism formulated in Schmidt; Ganz (2016) is no longer sufficient, as will be explained in detail:

„Generally speaking, narcissism (from an analytical perspective) is a reaction to the fear of losing a loved reference object that has already been experienced and is therefore feared again in the future. A strong personality architecture (i.e. usually an already differentiated and adult P) can allow this fear, and if necessary also show it appropriately to the outside world and deal with it. A weaker personality, for example a child in its early development phase, perceives this loss as an existential threat that it cannot counteract. In order to deal with this indirectly (= neurotically), it begins to devalue the reference object a priori and to increase its value in order to keep the damage to itself as low as possible in the event of a loss of the relationship."

In order to achieve a differentiated understanding of pathogenesis, the previously described dogmas of the we- and culture-less I must be eliminated. Just like the dogmatic walls that separate humans from animals, the natural sciences from the humanities, and their various disciplines from one another. Not as legitimate and necessary fictions in the sense of Vaihinger (Vaihinger, Hans 1923), but as iron curtains.

„We have protecting walls enough. We need more bridges."
(Wagoner et al. 2021)

For this purpose, the theories of psychologist Fyodor Vasilyuk and three scientists, none of whom are psychologists in the true sense of the word, will be used and combined.
• Lev Vygotsky – was actually a literary scholar and only came to psychology because of the upheavals caused by the Russian Revolution and the First World War.
• Aaron Antonovsky – was a medical sociologist, and
• Etienne Wenger – is a sociologist of knowledge.
The theories of Antonovsky and Wenger will not only be combined, but "transposed" from sociology to psychonomy. And this will be done with an extension – not included in the original versions – primarily to the area of the unconscious. The unconscious not in the sense defined by Freud, but by Hassin et al. (2005), among others.

15.1   From Outside to Inside – Vygotsky

Lev Vygotsky vehemently opposes the dogma of a solipsistic, self-developing ego, as already presented.

"The actual process of development of children's thinking does not occur from individual to socialized, but from social to individual thinking. This is the main result of both the theoretical and experimental study of the problem we are interested in."
(Vygotsky, L. 2017)

According to Vygotsky and his colleagues, a child's development proceeds in exactly the reverse order, from the outside to the inside. From the first breath, the child begins to interact with the world, and not only after overcoming primary narcissism or autism.

"A decisive step towards bridging the gap between the internal and the external was achieved by L. S. Vygotsky, A, V. Zaporozhets, A. N. Leontiev, A. R. Luria, S. L. Rubinstein, and their pupils and successors, who laid the foundations for construction of a psychological theory of activity. According to this theory, the emergence of a mediated structure of psychological processes in the human being is the result of the social activity of that being. Mental processes are born of activity, and become functional organs of activity. The theory was originally developed on the basis of material concerning cognitive processes—perception, attention, memory, thought. Within the framework of this theory these processes are seen as particular forms of perceptive, mnemonic and mental actions, which pass through a long period of development." (Vasilyuk, F. 1988)

„The point is that there is no adaptation to objective reality for the sake of adaptation itself - regardless of the needs of the organism or personality. All adaptation to reality is directed by needs. This is quite banal, a truism that somehow incomprehensibly got lost sight of in the theory under consideration. Essential to this problem in Piaget's theory is the separation of the biological and the social. The biological is understood as the original, primary, contained in the child itself, which forms its psychic substance. The social acts through coercion as an external force that is foreign to the child, which displaces the child's own thought processes and corresponds to its inner nature and replaces them with thought patterns that are foreign to the child and imposed from outside. It is therefore not surprising that even in his new scheme Piaget connects the two extreme points - egocentrism and cooperation - with a third link - coercion. This is the right word to describe Piaget's idea of the mechanism by which the social environment guides the development of a child's thinking.

In fact, Piaget shares this idea with psychoanalysis, which also sees the external environment as something external to the personality, which puts pressure on the personality, forcing it to limit, change and orient itself in a roundabout way. Coercion and pressure - these are the two words that constantly appear in the pages of the book when it comes to the influence of the social environment on the child's development.

This idea is not exclusive to Piaget. All theories in child psychology that start from the same fundamental positions as Piaget are permeated by it. The child lives in two worlds, everything social is alien to the child, imposed from outside." (Vygotskij, L. 2017)

Vygotsky, on the other hand, sees the development of the child as a continuous process of interaction with the social environment. Aaron Antonovsky examined this process of interaction and of the results with regard to the question of how health develops, how "salutogenesis" occurs.

15.2   Antonovsky – Sense of Coherence (SOC)

In search of answers to the question of why people react differently in the same stressful circumstances (for example in a concentration camp) - some get sick, others don't - the medical sociologist Aaron Antonovsky developed the concept of the "sense of coherence". This is made up of three components:

- Understandability
- Manageability
- Significance

According to Antonovsky (1997), people with a high sense of coherence have a high level of resilience to negative environmental situations.

Although Antonovsky assumed that these three areas develop in childhood, he did not investigate or treat this further.

Antonovsky therefore does not look at pathogenesis, but rather *salutogenesis*, i.e. the development of health.

He starts from the end point and summarizes this as follows:

„Die Hauptthese des salutogenetischen Modells ist, dass ein starkes SOC entscheidend für erfolgreiches Coping mit den allgegenwärtigen Stressoren des Lebens und damit für den Erhalt der Gesundheit ist." (Antonovsky, Aaron 1997)[79]

Antonovsky also follows a psychological-cognitive approach, not a psychonomic one (see foreword).

Before the presentation, an example of the three areas of comprehensibility, manageability and significance from a psychonomic perspective is therefore presented as a contrast.

When an elephant is born, the herd comes together to welcome the newcomer and accept him into the herd. The baby elephant thus gains "legitimate peripheral participation" in a "community of practice" (Wenger, E. 1998)[80].

---

[79] "The main thesis of the salutogenic model is that a strong SOC is crucial for successfully coping with the omnipresent stressors of life and thus for maintaining health." (Antonovsky, Aaron 1997)

[80] It should be noted, however, that Wenger also advocates a rational-conscious approach and ignores unconscious processes.

The baby elephant achieves "understandability" primarily through the "negotiation of meaning" (Wenger, E. 1998) with the mother and the rest of the herd as a "community of practice", whereby the baby elephant primarily adopts/learns the meaning framework of the mother and the herd.

In adolescence, the development of manageability is then in the foreground, even if the times in which understandability and manageability are developed cannot be clearly separated from one another and naturally influence one another.

The significance grows as a result. Namely, the significance for the herd. An elephant cow becomes the bearer and mediator of meaning. In the extreme form as a lead cow, whose decisions have a direct meaning that is relevant to the survival of the herd (an interpretation of the physical and social environment and actions derived from it).

The human baby also develops "understandability" from the first breath in interaction with the physical and social environment, with a "community of practice" (Wenger, Etienne), not only after the development of cognitive skills.

On the contrary, cognitive skills develop on the basis of learning abilities, but in active (!) engagement with the environment.

And it is childhood in which vulnerability is greatest, because the child (in contrast to the dogma of the solipsistic, we-less I) is still dependent on the social environment in developing the three components of the SOC.

However, the three levels of comprehensibility, manageability and significance always remain in a dynamic relationship with the environment - so they can also decline or disappear completely. An example of this is long-term prisoners who first have to be "resocialized" because they have lost the ability to understand the world outside of prison.

15.2.a   Comprehensibility

Antonovsky defines understandability as follows:

„Verstehbarkeit ist in der Tat der gut definierte, explizite Kern der ursprünglichen Definition. Sie bezieht sich auf das Ausmaß, in welchem man interne und externe Stimuli als kognitiv sinnhaft wahrnimmt, als geordnete, konsistente, strukturierte und klare Information und nicht als Rauschen – chaotisch, ungeordnet, willkürlich, zufällig und unerklärlich."
(Antonovsky, Aaron 1997)[81]

But comprehensibility is also, but not only, passively tied to the outside. Understanding is achieved primarily through activity and interaction with the environment.
And it is also actively created, as shown in the most important study by B. F. Skinner (1948), "Superstition in the pigeon".
The pigeon in the Skinner box tries to assign a dependency on its behavior to the feeding controlled by a random generator, in other words to create order.
And, as Etienne Wenger shows, "comprehensibility" is created by the social negotiation of meaning in communities of practice. This will be explained in more detail in the relevant paragraph.

15.2.b   Manageability

„… diese zweite Komponente Handhabbarkeit und definierte sie formal als das Ausmaß, in dem man wahrnimmt, daß man

---

81   "Indeed, comprehensibility is the well-defined, explicit core of the original definition. It refers to the extent to which one perceives internal and external stimuli as cognitively meaningful, as ordered, consistent, structured and clear information, rather than as noise - chaotic, disordered, arbitrary, random and inexplicable." (Antonovsky, Aaron 1997)

geeignete Ressourcen zur Verfügung hat, um den Anforderungen zu begegnen, die von den Stimuli, mit denen man konfrontiert wird, ausgehen. „Zur Verfügung" stehen Ressourcen, die man selbst unter Kontrolle hat oder solche, die von legitimierten anderen kontrolliert werden – vom Ehepartner, von Freunden, Kollegen, Gott, der Geschichte, vom Parteiführer oder einem Arzt – von jemandem, auf den man zählen kann, jemandem, dem man vertraut." (Antonovsky, Aaron 1997)[82]

Understandability and manageability develop together, influencing each other, through active engagement with reality - not just social reality. They are based at least in part on consistent feedback from the environment. The development of both understandability and manageability is at least made more difficult by both missing and inconsistent feedback.
To shed more light on the emergence of manageability, we will use Fyodor Vasilyuk's theory of "experiencing" in a separate chapter.

15.2.c   Significance

„Die dritte Komponente, Bedeutsamkeit, deutete sich ebenfalls in der ursprünglichen Diskussion an, als ich vor „einer zu starken Betonung des kognitiven Aspekts des Kohärenzgefühls" (1979, S. 127) warnte und darauf verwies, wie wichtig es ist, „als Teilnehmer in die Prozesse, die das eigene Schicksal und die alltägliche Erfahrung bilden", (S. 128) involviert zu sein.

---

82   "... this second component, manageability, and formally defined it as the extent to which one perceives that one has appropriate resources available to meet the demands posed by the stimuli one is confronted with. "Available" are resources that one has control over oneself or those that are controlled by legitimate others - one's spouse, friends, colleagues, God, history, the party leader or a doctor - someone one can count on, someone one trusts." (Antonovsky, Aaron 1997)

… Diejenigen, die nach unserer Einteilung ein starkes SOC hatten, sprachen immer von Lebensbereichen, die ihnen wichtig waren, die ihnen sehr am Herzen lagen, die in ihren Augen „Sinn machten" und zwar in der emotionalen, nicht nur der kognitiven Bedeutung des Terminus. Ereignisse, die sich in diesen Bereichen abspielten, wurden tendenziell als Herausforderung und als wichtig genug angesehen, emotional in sie zu investieren und sich zu engagieren." (Antonovsky, Aaron 1997)[83]

The example of the elephant showed that there is definitely another, evolutionarily more meaningful interpretation of significance. It is the significance for others that has arisen through years of dealing with and acting in reality.

"Significance" is based on the existence, i.e. the dynamic development, of meaning, a meaning framework. The meaning is, as already mentioned and will be presented in more detail, negotiated in activity communities (Wenger, E.).

15.2.d   Resources

"Mir scheint eindeutig, daß ein hohes Ausmaß an Handhabbarkeit stark von einem hohen Maß an Verstehbarkeit abhängt. Eine Voraussetzung für das Gefühl, daß man über Ressourcen verfügt, um vor Anforderungen bestehen zu können, ist, daß

---

83   "The third component, meaningfulness, was also hinted at in the original discussion when I warned against "too much emphasis on the cognitive aspect of the sense of coherence" (1979, p. 127) and pointed out the importance of being involved "as participants in the processes that shape one's destiny and everyday experience" (p. 128). … Those who, according to our classification, had a strong SOC always spoke of areas of life that were important to them, that were very dear to them, that "made sense" to them in the emotional, not just the cognitive, sense of the term. Events that took place in these areas tended to be viewed as challenging and important enough to invest in and engage in emotionally." (Antonovsky, Aaron 1997)

man eine klare Vorstellung von eben diesen Anforderungen hat. In einer Welt zu leben, die man für chaotisch und unberechenbar hält, macht es höchst schwer zu glauben, daß man gut zurecht kommt." (Antonovsky, A. 1997)[84]

„Zusammengefaßt: die wahrgenommenen Ressourcen sind der Schlüssel zu dem Problem der Überlastung. Aber die fraglichen Ressourcen können auch kollektiv oder außerhalb des Individuums sein. Was das Erleben der Handhabbarkeit einschränkt, ist chronische oder häufig wiederholte akute Überlastung ohne die angemessene Gelegenheit zu Ruhe und Erholung. Überlastung bleibt das wichtigste Thema in Hinblick auf Handhabbarkeit, …" (Antonovsky, A. 1997)[85]

Here again, the cognitively conscious aspect is in the foreground. However, the development of resources begins at a time in the child when the cognitive functions are not yet fully developed and are at their most vulnerable.
In order to understand the pathogenesis of narcissistic personality disorders, it is necessary to perceive the dynamic and reciprocal development of comprehensibility and manageability as an activity, as well as the resources resulting from this.

---

84 "It seems clear to me that a high degree of manageability depends heavily on a high degree of understandability. A prerequisite for feeling that one has the resources to cope with challenges is having a clear idea of what those challenges are. Living in a world that one considers chaotic and unpredictable makes it extremely difficult to believe that one is coping well." (Antonovsky, A. 1997)

85 "In summary, perceived resources are the key to the problem of overload. But the resources in question can also be collective or external to the individual. What limits the experience of manageability is chronic or frequently repeated acute overload without adequate opportunity for rest and recovery. Overload remains the most important issue with regard to manageability, ..." (Antonovsky, A. 1997)

15.2.e   rigid SOC / strong SOC

„Die Person mit einem rigiden SOC hält an Koestlers Kanon bzw. Gatlins gespeicherter Information fest. Die Person mit einem starken SOC sucht nach einer Balance zwischen Regeln und Strategien, zwischen gespeicherter und potentieller Information. Sie vertraut darauf, daß mit der neuen Information etwas Sinnvolles anzulangen ist. Sie empfindet kaum eine Gefahr dabei, die Welt als Herausforderung zu betrachten und Feedback gegenüber aufgeschlossen zu sein."
(Antonovsky, A. 1997)[86]

A rigid SOC is characteristic of people with narcissistic personality disorder. The refusal to perceive reality, in connection with and as a necessary consequence, the impossibility of re-evaluating it.
Narcissists develop a pseudo-SOC[87], a sense of coherence independent of reality, based on the construction of their own, unrealistic kingdom, which does not offer the possibility of re-evaluating reality and thus changing action strategies.

15.2.f   Stresses

"Die Welt der Bewußtseinswirklichkeit, unsres Wachens Welt, ist: die Welt der Notstände und des Ausgleichs dieser Notstände." (Lessing, Th. 1929/2021)[88]

---

86   "The person with a rigid SOC sticks to Koestler's canon or Gatlin's stored information. The person with a strong SOC looks for a balance between rules and strategies, between stored and potential information. They trust that something useful can be achieved with the new information. They hardly feel any danger in seeing the world as a challenge and being open to feedback." (Antonovsky, A. 1997)

87   See also: Schmidt, B.; Ganz, A. (2016)

Under the meaning framework of a solipsistic ego that develops from within itself, the importance of interaction in general and stressful interactions in particular is overlooked.

It is not Freudian libidinal drives, but real challenges of reality that must be mastered, at least outside of affluent society.

If this mastery is successful again and again, a high level of resilience to new challenges develops, not despite but precisely because of the existing stressors.

"... , daß ein hohes Ausmaß an Stressoren bei gleichzeitigem hohen Ausmaß an sozialer Unterstützung gesundheitsfördernd ist; ..." (Antonovsky, A. 1997)[89]

The Western concept of a we-, culture- and body-less self, as described above, has ignored the fact that people are, above all, one thing: social beings.

In other words, beings who need social community and shared activity both for their development from the first breath and to overcome "stressors".

15.3   Communities of Practice – Wenger

There are clear parallels between Etienne Wenger's theory and the cultural-historical activity theory of Lev Vygotsky and his colleagues. Learning and the formation of identity is not understood as a solipsistic self, but rather through activity, the negotiation within a socio-cultural environment.

So while Vygotsky describes the direction of the child's development, from the outside to the inside, and Antonovsky descri-

---

88   "The world of conscious reality, the world of our waking life, is: the world of emergencies and the balancing of these emergencies." (Lessing, Th. 1929/2021)

89   "... that a high level of stressors combined with a high level of social support is beneficial to health; ..." (Antonovsky, A. 1997)

bes the importance of the comprehensibility of the environment for the development of manageability, significance and thus the SOC, Wenger explains how comprehensibility and thus also manageability are developed.

„Communities of Practice presents a theory of learning that starts with this assumption: engagement in social practice is the fundamental process by which we learn and so become who we are. The primary unit of analysis is neither the individual nor social institutions but rather the informal "communities of practice" that people form as they pursue shared enterprises over time. In order to give a social account of learning, the theory explores in a systematic way the intersection of issues of community, social practice, meaning, and identity. The result is a broad conceptual framework for thinking about learning as a process of social participation." (Wenger, E. 1998/2016)

Meaning does not simply lie outside, as decontextualized phi-losophical theories assume, but is assigned to things and events.
These assignments, these meaning frameworks, are socially mediated through shared activity; they are negotiated and thus shape the entire person.

„It implied emphasis on comprehensive understanding invol-ving the whole person rather than "receiving" a body of factual knowledge about the world; on activity in and with the world; and on the view that agent, activity, and the world mutually constitute each other." (Lave, J.; Wenger, E. 1991)

„Our attempts to understand human life open a vast space of relevant questions — from the origin of the universe to the workings of the brain, from the details of every thought to the

117

purpose of life. In this vast space of questions, the concept of practice is useful for addressing a specific slice; a focus on the experience of meaningfulness. Practice is, first and foremost, a process by which we can experience the world and our engagement with it as meaningful." (Wenger, E. 1998/2016)

Etienne Wenger's theory contains three aspects that are particularly interesting for understanding comprehensibility:
1. Learning does not occur individually, but through active participation in "communities of practice". In these, meaning is negotiated (negotiation of meaning).
2. Participation develops slowly from "legitimate peripheral participation" to "full participant in a sociocultural practice".
3. Personal identity develops through participation in the "negotiation of meaning".

„A social theory of learning must therefore integrate the components necessary to characterize social participation as a process of learning and of knowing. These components, ..., include the following.
1) Meaning: a way of talking about our (changing) ability – individually and collectively – to experience our life and the world as meaningful.
2) Practice: a way of talking about the shared historical and social resources, frameworks, and perspectives that can sustain mutual engagement in action.
3) Community: a way of talking about the social configurations in which our enterprises are defined as worth pursuing and our participation is recognizable as competence.
4) Identity: a way of talking about how learning changes who we are and creates personal histories of becoming in the context of our communities." (Wenger, E. 1998/2016)

15.3.a Communities of Practice

The theory of "Communities of Practice" includes the points "community", "practice" and "negotiation of meaning" within the *community* and through *practice*.

„Because the term „community" is usually a very positive one, I cannot emphasize enough that these interrelations arise out of engagement in practice and not out of an idealized view of what a community should be like. In particular, connotations of peaceful coexistence, mutual support, or interpersonal allegiance are not assumed, though of course they may exist in specific cases. Peace, happiness, and harmony are therefore not necessary properties of a community of practice."
(Wenger, E. 1998/2016)

Neither the activities nor the negotiation of meaning have to be conflict-free or harmonious. We will see from Vasilyuk that it is the critical, actually unmanageable experiences that teach us the most.

„The concept of practice connotes doing, but not just doing in and of itself It is doing in a historical and social context that gives structure and meaning to what we do. In this sense, practice is always social practice.
Such a concept of practice includes both the explicit and the tacit. It includes what is said and what is left unsaid; what is represented and what is assumed. It includes the language, tools, documents, images, symbols, well-defined roles, specified criteria, codified procedures, regulations, and contracts that various practices make explicit for a variety of purposes. But it also includes all the implicit relations, tacit conventions, subtle cues, untold rules of thumb, recognizable intuitions. specific

perceptions, well-tuned sensitivities, embodied understandings, underlying assumptions, and shared world views. Most of these may never be articulated, yet they are unmistakable signs of membership in communities of practice and are crucial to the success of their enterprises." (Wenger, E. 1998/2016)

The negotiation of meaning through activity always takes place within a cultural framework, or, in other words, within a psychonomic species.

„Being alive as human beings means that we are constantly engaged in the pursuit of enterprises of all kinds, from ensuring our physical survival to seeking the most lofty pleasures. As we define these enterprises and engage in their pursuit together, we interact with each other and with the world and we tune our relations with each other and with the world accordingly. In other words, we learn. Over time, this collective learning results in practices that reflect both the pursuit of our enterprises and the attendant social relations. These practices are thus the property of a kind of community created over time by the sustained pursuit of a shared enterprise. It makes sense, therefore, to call these kinds of communities communities of practice.
In this sense, living is a constant process of negotiation of meaning." (Wenger, E. 1998/2016)

„The negotiation of meaning may involve language, but it is not limited to it. It includes our social relations as factors in the negotiation, but it does not necessarily involve a conversation or even direct interaction with other human beings. The concept of negotiation often denotes reaching an agreement between people, as in „negotiating a price," but it is not limited to that usage. It is also used to suggest an accomplishment that requires sustained attention and readjustment, as in „negotiating a sharp curve." I want to capture both aspects at once in order to suggest that living meaningfully implies:

1) an active process of producing meaning that is both dynamic and historical

2) a world of both resistance and malleability

3) the mutual ability to affect and to be affected

4) the engagement of a multiplicity of factors and perspectives

5) the production of a new resolution to the convergence of these factors and perspectives

6) the incompleteness of this resolution, which can be partial, tentative, ephemeral, and specific to a situation."

(Wenger, E. 1998/2016)

Ontogeny therefore takes place through activity within a cultural-historical-social environment.

15.3.b   Legitimate Peripheral Participation

„Learning viewed as situated activity has as its central defining characteristic a process that we call legitimate peripheral participation. By this we mean to draw attention to the point that learners inevitably participate in communities of practitioners and that the mastery of knowledge and skill requires newcomers to move toward full participation in the sociocultural practices of a community.

"Legitimate peripheral participation" provides a way to speak about the relations between newcomers and old-timers, and about activities, identities, artifacts, and communities of knowledge and practice. It concerns the process by which newcomers become part of a community of practice. A person's intentions to learn are engaged and the meaning of learning is configured through the process of becoming a full participant in a sociocultural practice. This social process includes, indeed it subsumes, the learning of knowledgeable skills." (Lave, J.; Wenger, E. 1991)

Children do not develop from within themselves, from the inside out, as assumed by Freud, Piaget and others, but rather they grow slowly through shared activity into the social environment of the meaning and action frameworks surrounding them.

"... children are, after all, quintessential legitimate peripheral participants in adult social worlds." (Lave, J.; Wenger, E. 1991)

15.3.c Identity

"Talking about identity in social terms is not denying individuality but vewing the very definition of individuality as something that is part of the practices of specific communities. It is therefore a mistaken dichotomy to wonder whether the unit of analysis of identity should be the community or the person. The focus must be on the process of their mutual constitution." (Wenger, E. 1998/2016)

"My discussion of the social formation of identities is not based on an assumption of either agreement or conflict. By refusing to assume an inherent divergence between the individual and the social, I am not saying that there is never any tension or conflict between the resources and demands of groups and the aspirations of individuals. In each specific case, there may be tensions, conflicts, or concessions; but, for every case where there is a conflict, you can find a case where individual and social developments enhance each other. Thus acknowledging that there can be specific tensions between individuals and collectivities is cry different from positing a dichotomy with a fundamental divergence between them." (Wenger, E. 1998/2016)

„The work of identity is always going on. Identity is not some primordial core of personality that already exists. Nor is it something we acquire at some point in the same way that, at a certain age, we grow a set of permanent teeth. Even though issues of identity as a focus of overt concern may become more salient at certain times than at others, our identity is something we constantly renegotiate during the course of our lives." (Wenger, E. 1998/2016)

15.4   Experiencing – Vasilyuk

Fyodor E. Vasilyuk builds on the activity theory of Vygotsky and his colleagues.

„A decisive step towards bridging the gap between the internal and the external was achieved by L. S. Vygotsky, A, V. Zaporozhets, A. N. Leontiev, A. R. Luria, S. L. Rubinstein, and their pupils and successors, who laid the foundations for construction of a psychological theory of activity. According to this theory, the emergence of a mediated structure of psychological processes in the human being is the result of the social activity of that being. Mental processes are born of activity, and become functional organs of activity. The theory was originally developed on the basis of material concerning cognitive processes—perception, attention, memory, thought. Within the framework of this theory these processes are seen as particular forms of perceptive, mnemonic and mental actions, which pass through a long period of development." (Vasilyuk, F. 1988)

Vasilyuk is of the opinion that it is particularly the challenges that go beyond what is manageable that allow a person to grow, creating what Antonovsky would call a strong SOC that is capable of reassessing things when circumstances change. Vasilyuk calls this process of dealing with seemingly insurmountable situations "experiencing".

„And yet we are obliged to reject the terms "psychological defence" and "coping behaviour", firstly because the categories they represent delimit only some partial aspects of the integral problem seen here, thus none of them can aspire to the role of general category; and secondly because the terms "defence" and "coping" have too many associations with psychoanalysis and behaviourism, whereas this study has been conducted along lines proper to a quite different school of psychology, that of Vygotsky, Leontiev and Luria, a school which in many ways stands opposed to psychoanalysis and behaviourism, but which in our opinion is potentially capable of assimilating all that is true in the concepts of the above-mentioned schools, and of making a major contribution towards creating a psychological theory of the processes through which critical situations are dealt with. For those reasons, then we need a new, fresh term. We have decided to use the term experiencing to denote the subject-matter of our study." (Vasilyuk, F. 1988)

Vasilyuk defines "Experiencing" as follows:

"The specifics of this activity are determined by the peculiarities of the situations which put the individual under the necessity of experiencing. We shall refer to these as critical situations. If one had to use one word only to define the nature of such situations one would have to say that they are situations of im-

possibility. Impossibility of what? Impossibility of living, of re-
alising the internal necessities of life.

The struggle against that impossibility, the struggle to realise
internal necessities—that is experiencing. Experiencing is the
repair of a "disruption" of life, a work of restoration, procee-
ding as it were at right angles to the line of actualisation of life.
If the psychological theory of activity studies, figuratively
speaking, the way in which a human being travels life's road,
then the theory of experiencing studies the way in which he or
she falls and rises again to continue the journey. The fact that
the processes of experiencing are counterposed to actualisation
of life, i.e., to activity, does not mean that they are mystical
processes taking place outside life; in their psychological constitution they are processes of life and activity like any others,
but in their psychological meaning and purpose they are processes acting upon life itself, to ensure the psychological possibility of actualising life. This is the most abstract formulation
of experiencing on the existential plane, abstracted, that is,
from consciousness." (Vasilyuk, F. 1988)

What once applied to kings and their children now applies to
more and more people in a society of excess - and especially
children:

"But since the king was not happy that his son was leaving the
controlled roads and wandering around the countryside to form
his own opinion of the world, he gave him a carriage and a horse. "Now you don't have to walk anymore," were his words.
"Now you aren't allowed to anymore," was their meaning.
"Now you can't anymore," was their effect!" (Günter Anders -
Children's Stories)[90]

---

90   See also: Levy, David M. (1943)

A hedonistic perception arises due to the increasing degrees of freedom, i.e. the lack of real challenges that necessarily have to be overcome.

15.4.a   Hedonistic Experiencing

„When the envelope of the easy and simple existence is torn open—that is the point from which we can approach the main object of our theoretical study, experiencing; here, the experiencing proper to the life-world just described. In that life-world taken in its pure form there is no place for experiencing, since its ease and simplicity, i.e., the fact that all life processes are provided for and contain no contradictions, exclude all possibility of any situations arising which call for experiencing. More than that, even when existence suddenly, for one reason or another, ceases to be easy and simple, and such situations do arise, the creature "educated" by the easy and simple world is not capable of experiencing in the true sense of the word. It is not capable of it because an essential premise of experiencing is the occurrence of ideational transformations of the psychological world (although experiencing is not reduced to them), and the creature under consideration is without any ideational characteristics at all. Its life is entirely material and corporeal, indeed essentially intra-corporeal, since its external contacts are limited to taking in needed substances and getting rid of unneeded ones, processes requiring no activity on its part. Being incapable of "responding" to a critical situation either by external practical activity or by ideational transformations in its psychological world, the creature responds by the only means available to it—changes within the body. These equate to the concept of physiological stress reactions." (Vasilyuk, F. 1988)

Here, Vasilyuk describes the core of the development of narcissistic personality disorders, which is made possible by the cultural freedoms of an affluent society.

And also describes the core of the narcissistic personality.

„Hedonistic experiencing ignores reality, distorts and denies it, creating an illusion of the need being actually satisfied, and more generally of the damaged content of life being still intact." (Vasilyuk, F. 1988)

16   Culture and Narcissism

If the question raised at the beginning about the connection between mental disorders and culture in its generality could not be answered, an answer to the question about the relationship between narcissism and culture, about the causes of the (supposed) increase in narcissistic personality disorders, is now possible. This was and is not possible under a solipsistic dogma. Humans, like many other "higher" animal species, come into the world as "cosmopolitan, curious creatures"[91] (Konrad Lorenz).

They do not react to the world passively using stimulus-response schemes, but actively explore the world. Even if this exploration can be associated with high risks.

Knowledge is acquired in advance, latently, regardless of current need. And through the mutual interaction between reality, social environment and the individual, the latter also develops resources for confronting stressors. On the one hand, through the development of comprehensibility and manageability according to Antonovsky, and also through experiencing according to Vasilyuk. These resources enable the maturing child to overcome ever greater challenges. If these resources are not de-

---

91   weltoffene Neugierwesen

veloped, regardless of which part of the interdependent influences they are caused by, a profound disturbance in the relationship to reality and the social environment occurs.

In summary, the previously mentioned symptom complex of narcissistic disorders can be traced back to the change from a cosmopolitan, curious being to a xenophobic and neophobic being who fears reality as a whole and therefore constructs his own "kingdom".

For many people, and not just kings etc., this is only possible within a culture that has distanced itself from nature or emancipated itself so much that this does not lead to immediate selection.

At the same time, it is this lack of feedback in general that prevents the development of resources through active engagement with the environment and makes it difficult to negotiate meaning and thus comprehensibility. This means that the feeling of both manageability and significance according to Antonovsky cannot develop.

There are therefore several paths open to the development of a narcissistic personality disorder.

17   Traumatization

In principle, a distinction must be made between singular traumas and continuous traumas. In other words, experiences that occur once and thus lead to traumatization, and those that occur more frequently or continuously. An example of the latter is the feeling of inferiority due to personal deficits, which Alfred Adler (e.g. 1912) used as the basis for his theory. Inferiority, however, is always a relative feeling in relation to the environment. For example, within an above-average intelligent family, a child with rather average abilities can feel inferior, although in other families he would perceive himself as a good average.

„Auch die körperliche Beeinträchtigung wirkt neuroseerzeugend nur auf dem Umweg über ihren Positionseffekt, als Anlass einer erlebten Unterlegenheit im Vergleich mit anderen. ... Voll verständlich wird dies erst durch die Klärung einer weiteren Bedeutung von 'Position'. Sie bedeutet nämlich nicht nur eine bestimmte Stelle in einem Koordinatensystem, sondern außerdem eine Zugehörigkeit oder Nichtzugehörigkeit zu einer Gruppe – und zu den anderen überhaupt – , das Innerhalb- oder Außerhalbsein, das Aufgenommen- oder Isoliertsein. Diese beiden Positionen sind zwei Verhaltensweisen des Menschen zugeordnet, die man am besten mit einem Ausdruck der vergleichenden Verhaltensforschung als "Freundverhalten" und "Feindverhalten" bezeichnet." (Adler, A. 1912)[92]

Resources and social support also play a central role in feelings of inferiority, as in the singular traumas discussed below.

Another factor to mention is either inconsistent or largely lacking consistent feedback from the mother/family members, which prevents the development of "understandability".

---

92 "Physical impairment also only causes neurosis indirectly via its position effect, as a reason for an experienced inferiority in comparison with others. ... This only becomes fully understandable when another meaning of 'position' is clarified. It does not only mean a specific place in a coordinate system, but also belonging or not belonging to a group - and to others in general -, being inside or outside, being accepted or isolated. These two positions are associated with two types of human behavior that are best described using a term from comparative behavioral research as 'friend behavior' and 'enemy behavior'." (Adler, A. 1912)

18   Resources and traumatization

Whether an experience becomes a trauma or not depends essentially on the resources available. Trauma only occurs when the experience demands far more than the resources available and there is insufficient social support.

Without activity in reality and the resulting feedback and challenges, and thus also the risk of situations that overtax resources, resources cannot be formed in the first place.

Contrary to the Western dogma of the solipsistic, self-developing ego, ontogenesis is based on social interaction based on the cultural environment.

The role of cultural factors is thus evident not only in ontogenesis, but also in pathogenesis.

19   Pathways of pathogenesis

The development of a narcissistic personality disorder through trauma is limited to early childhood.

In this period, the child, starting with the interaction between him and the mother or primary caregiver, builds up the comprehensibility and manageability, the appropriate framework of meaning.

The interaction with the social environment expands constantly, first to the family circle and then to an ever larger part of reality, and so on.

If necessary parts (consistent feedback, social support...) are missing in this development process, the necessary resources are not built up. The risk of trauma increases, resulting in anxiety of reality.

However, we are not only afraid of what we have come to know as threatening, but also of what we have not come to know (xenophobia, neophobia).

Anxiety[93] disrupts further interaction with reality and the social environment, and thus the "negotiation of meaning" as well as the development of one's own social identity.

Different paths to traumatization must be distinguished.

19.1   Critical situation cannot be managed

On the one hand, critical situations lead to trauma that cannot be overcome. A distinction must be made here between those that cannot be overcome objectively and those that cannot be overcome subjectively.

19.1.a   Objective

There are experiences in life that are so massive that no amount of resources or social support, no matter how intensive, would be enough to cope with them. These situations are objectively critical situations because no person of the same age, no matter how good their resources, can cope with them.

19.1.b   Subjective

At the same time, however, there are also situations that could be managed but the necessary resources or social support are lacking. These are subjective critical situations because the resources needed to deal with them are not available to the individual.

As already shown, the resources needed to deal with crises are created, among other things, by the feeling of being understood (Antonovsky).

---

93   To understand this, it is necessary to distinguish between fear and anxiety. Fear is caused by the unknown and is accompanied by more or less curiosity. Anxiety, on the other hand, leads to avoidance behavior.

The increasing degree of freedom in an affluent society emancipated from nature and social traditions is, however, in principle accompanied by a reduction in understandability. The separation from nature and the change to an artificial environment that is changing ever more rapidly makes orientation more difficult, as practical activities in a natural environment are hardly possible anymore and the corresponding feedback is lacking. The social traditions used to offer orientation, just as the family structures of extended families compensated for problems of the parents, for example. The reduction to small families prevents the cross-generational balancing of idiosyncratic problems.

The problems of the parents can therefore more easily lead to problems of the children.

"The same goal of a constant need for self-affirmation is also apparent in various clinical writings, which in addition provide some suggestions for its origin. In one way or another, they all in essence describe narcissists as individuals whose self-needs in childhood were not met due to deficiencies in early parental empathy or neglect, and who thus seek to fulfill these needs in their adult relationships. For example, Kernberg (1975) ascribed the disorder to a rejecting mother and the child's subsequent feelings of abandonment. Kohut (1971, 1972) pointed to inconsistent and capricious reinforcement, highly dependent on the mother's mood; and Millon (1981) blamed constant overvaluation that is not based on any objective reality. Thus, although the clinical theorists disagree about the exact etiology, they all see the origins of the fragile but grandiose self as a response to unempathetic and inconsistent early childhood interactions." (Morf, Rhodewalt 2001)

However, the question remains whether the influence of the parents/mothers is primary or secondary, because the disturbed child-parent relationship does not allow the necessary resources in Antonovsky's sense to be built up, since the child does not receive consistent feedback from the parents.

19.2 Critical situations do not have to be dealt with

In contrast to situations that cannot be dealt with subjectively or objectively, in a society of excess there is an increasing possibility of not having to deal with critical situations, of simply avoiding them.

"Princely children do not learn anything thoroughly, except perhaps how to ride: the horse is neither a flatterer nor a court entourage and is just as likely to throw off the king's son as the son of the cart pusher." (Montaigne, Michel de)

The problem of princely children is becoming a general problem. If the nomad child in the steppe had to get back on the horse that it had previously thrown off, it would now be easy to switch to an e-scooter. Or the child is driven in the parents' SUV.
However, the experience of being thrown off remains unresolved, becomes traumatic, and thus horses and riding are filled with anxiety. The lack of necessity to confront and deal with critical situations prevents the development of resources on the one hand, and on the other hand continuously leads to an ever-increasing anxiety of reality.

20   Dissociation

The central point in understanding narcissistic personality disorder is the accompanying dissociative identity disorder.

Here too, understanding was prevented by the dogmatic positions of the past. Therefore, a new perspective on dissociations is necessary.

20.1   Excursus: Brain, Ego and Dissociation

The culturally and historically conditioned separation into humanities and natural sciences[94] postulates that the mind, the conscious self, has nothing to do with the body.

If one now approaches the question of the conditions and causes of the conscious self from the side of the humanities, i.e. philosophy and psychology, then the self apparently has a brain. In other words, the one, indivisible, "true" self that was originally breathed into us by God. From this perspective, it is of course almost impossible to understand the nature of dissociation, even if it is certainly perceived.

If one approaches the question from the side of biology, however, as George John Romanes (1885/2021) and Lloyd C. Morgan (1894/2005) have already done, then the conscious self is the result of an evolutionary development. A development from the rudimentary perception of stimuli in single-celled organisms, through increasingly complex processing of more and more stimuli in decentralized nervous systems, to our CNS.

The aim of this development was and is to be able to react better to the environment by integrating and processing more and more stimuli.

From this perspective, our conscious self appears as another or-

---

94   See also: Schmidt, Bernhard J. (2020b): Entwurf einer wissenschaftlichen Psychologie.

gan for interacting with the environment. And only from this perspective can dissociation be understood as an adaptive response.

As a reaction to the traumatic experience, whether continuous or occasional, contact with reality and thus the formation of a social identity within a "community of practice" (Wenger) is disrupted. The brain forms one or more new selves, whereby the original self as the primary personality remains at a childlike level but does not develop further.

This process is comparable to the formation of autonomous languages among twins or close siblings when there is no adequate language model.

„The prototypical situation is one in which two or more close siblings (not necessarily twins) grow up closely together during the language acquisition period. If an adult model language is frequently absent, the children use each other as a model and acquire the language imperfectly. The language may stabilise at that level.
If a model is completely absent, the children probably do not create a language." (Bakker, Peter 1987)

Unlike language development, new, individual personalities emerge in narcissistic personality disorder.

As already explained in Schmidt, B. (2020b), there is an urgent need to overcome the dogmatic separation of body and mind, of humanities and natural sciences.

20.2   Dissociation in Narcissism

"Narcissists fascinate many of us, because they appear to possess such an incongruous set of characteristics and perhaps because they seem like adult versions of infantile characteristics most people leave behind early in the course of development." (Morf; Rhodewalt 2001)

Morf and Rhodewalt describe the dissociative personality structure of narcissists very well, but without recognizing it. The dissociative structure consists of at least two, sometimes several personalities.

20.3   Primary personality

The primary personality remains intact in narcissists, but remains socio-emotionally at a childlike level, as this personality is cut off from further participation in the confrontation with reality or is protected from it (by the gatekeeper personality). The primary personality sometimes comes to the fore in very safe and protected situations and then surprises with its childlike naivety, which may not fit the person's biological age at all. At the same time, however, narcissists also use this to manipulate their counterparts. As ethologists know, courtship behavior always contains infantile behavior.

20.4   Narcissistic personality(s)

In addition to the primary personality, one or more narcissistic personalities form as new "organs" that construct their own "realities", actually illusory worlds. The kingdoms of the "king", in which he must always be superior to everyone, always competent and unassailable.

These personalities can be very different and can be activated for specific situations.

The essential characteristic of the narcissistic personality is that it lives in its own illusory world, in its own kingdom, which is turned away from reality.

The "negotiation of meaning" comes to a standstill, as does the building up of resources.

The narcissistic personality embodies the lonely king, cut off from feedback from reality.

The king who always has to be superior to everyone and always has to control everything. For whom social interaction, in the positive sense, is not possible. For whom everything is just a means and nothing is an end in itself.

The gatekeeper personality is also often found.

20.4.a   Gatekeeper

The gatekeeper protects the ego and acts vehemently and aggressively whenever the primary ego is supposedly threatened.

"A grandiose yet vulnerable self-concept appears to underlie the chronic goal of obtaining continuous external self-affirmation. Because narcissists are insensitive to others' concerns and social constraints and view others as inferior, their self-regulatory efforts often are counterproductive and ultimately prevent the positive feedback that they seek—thus undermining the self they are trying to create and maintain."
(Morf; Rhodewalt 2001)

The situations perceived as a threat do not have to be objectively dangerous, but only involve, for example, direct contact with reality, which is always a threat to one's own false world.

The gatekeeper often appears when the relationship with another person is no longer based purely on dependency and manipulation, but a real emotional relationship is developing, or existing dependencies (see the chapter on emotional and/or financial dependency) are threatened.

The relationship with other people would be a source of self-affirmation, but at the same time it is also a confrontation with reality and therefore a threat to the maintenance of one's own false world.

The relationship with other people requires that they be viewed as an end in themselves, and not just as a means.

For narcissists, however, other people always exist ONLY as a means, even their own children (Schmidt, B. 2020c).

21 Maintaining the illusion

For the narcissistic personality, dealing with reality without anxiety is not possible. The aim of all efforts, with all available energy, is to maintain one's own false world, one's own kingdom.

It has already been shown that this was previously only possible for a few people, but today, due to the affluent society, it is possible for many people.

21.1 Comfort zone / golden cage

The "cosmopolitan, curious being" (Konrad Lorenz) explores the world, tries new paths, takes risks.

The narcissistic personality, on the other hand, fears reality and therefore remains in the comfort zone of their own false world. But this comfort zone is also a golden cage[95] and, above all, limits personality development or makes it impossible.

Since narcissists do not want to or cannot leave their golden ca-

---

95   But the golden cage is also a personal hell.

ge, but need other people as vassals, they have to lure them into their golden cage, their false world.

21.1.a   Means / end

If one follows Kant's instruction to never view fellow human beings only as a means but always as an end in themselves, then this requires an engagement with reality and also with one's own identity in relation to fellow human beings. However, since this is not possible for narcissists, everything and everyone is abused as a means (Schmidt, B. 2020c, 2022). The exploitation of humans and nature is based on treating them only as a means.

And it occurs in "antagonistic symbiotic narcissism" (Schmidt, B.; Ganz, A. 2017). On the one hand, for example, as factory farming, in which animals only serve as a means, and on the other hand as pseudo-empathetic animal protection (Schmidt, B. 2022), in which the welfare of animals is declared to be the sole purpose. But even for the supposed animal rights activists, who themselves mistreat animals for years, animals are only a means of satisfying their narcissistic needs.

And, to stay with this example, in the further processing, i.e. the slaughter and processing of animals, the narcissistic perception is only found as a means in the exploitation of Eastern European temporary workers, the processing and relabeling of rotten meat, etc.

21.2   Orientation and effectiveness

Orientation towards reality is not possible; it must be independent of reality, which can lead to fatal errors.

At the same time, however, the need for effectiveness must be satisfied, so avoiding any activity is impossible.

Without the possibility of orientation towards reality, the satisfaction of the need for effectiveness, for significance, is usually destructive.

Narcissists are recognized less by what they do than by what they do not do - namely, the necessary and meaningful things. On the contrary, as is often observed with managers, the meaningful things are abolished and meaningful structures changed because the meaning of these is not recognized.

One can observe "displacement activities", such as the manager of a large hospital who walked through the corridors in the evening to turn off the lights, ignoring the insignificance of the costs saved in comparison to the total costs.

At the same time, the compulsion to bring everything under one's own control, to dominate everything, is overwhelming. Narcissists always have to be superior to everyone and everything in their kingdom, if only because of the narcissistic feeling of moral superiority.

21.3   Self-proclaimed experts

The easiest way for narcissists to become effective and self-affirmed, while at the same time avoiding the necessary confrontation with reality, is to declare themselves experts. And to develop pseudo-empathy in the areas in which they have declared themselves experts. For example, there are the animal rights activists in animal shelters who supposedly act to protect animals and, in accordance with the Animal Welfare Act, are against keeping dogs in kennels, i.e. do not place them in kennels. But they themselves have kept dogs in kennels in their animal shelters for many years (Schmidt, B. 2022).

The reality in relation to their own actions is ignored, and the animals are only abused as a means of satisfying narcissistic needs.

It is the esoterics who deny reality and rational explanations and, by appealing to "old knowledge", want to "heal" other people, "send energy", etc. after attending a few courses, ignoring the limitations of their own abilities.[96].

21.4   Power imbalance

Structures with dependency relationships and/or power imbalances are suitable for maintaining one's own false world with comparatively little risk, such as when escaping to the therapeutic meta-level, such as with consultants of all stripes, psychotherapists, etc.

The therapeutic meta-level separates therapists and consultants from reality, making them exalted and powerful.

These are positions with a pronounced power imbalance, such as with administrative employees, and/or dependency relationships with clients, such as with employees of youth welfare offices. Officials and administrative employees are always right in their own opinion, and work in an apparent world of laws and regulations - acting in a way that is out of touch with the world. And they always have the means at hand to bully and harass other people. And if reality and regulations don't match, what bad luck for reality.

Even if there are hardly any kings left, Mumford's statement still often applies to civil servants:

„Allzu oft identifizierten sich, wie die Dokumente zeigen, die Beamten, die die Anordnungen des Königs ausführten, mit der Quelle der Autorität und übertrieben die königliche Arroganz, ohne sie durch königliche Gnade zu kompensieren." (Mumford, L. 1986)[97]

---

96   See also: Wolfe, Tom (1976) und Tyler, Imogen (2007)

It is therefore not surprising that youth welfare offices are repeatedly criticized because, on the one hand, they often take unnecessary action, e.g. by taking children into care[98], but on the other hand, despite warnings, they do not prevent long-term child abuse. It is the combination of denial of reality and satisfaction of the need for effectiveness that leads to irrational and destructive behavior, made possible by dependency structures and power imbalances.

21.5   Overestimation of one's own worth

The "grandiose self" is a necessary characteristic of the "king". Without a developed, socially educated, realistic identity (Wenger, E.), the only remaining position is that of the "king", who is superior to everyone and anyone. And expects the corresponding homage and attention - without any real basis.

In order to maintain self-esteem, relationships, whether professional or private, are not established in any way based on competence. Competence is more of a hindrance because the competence of others represents a threat to one's own, exaggerated self-esteem. In contrast, the supposedly "suitable" employee is the incompetent one. He is preferred, promoted, etc.

Fools are also preferred in private relationships. The question of why someone surrounds themselves with people even though they are all "idiots" can be answered by changing from "although" to "because". Not although they are fools, but because they are, and thus do not represent any threat to one's own self-esteem.

---

97   "All too often, as the documents show, the officials who carried out the king's orders identified themselves with the source of authority and exaggerated royal arrogance without compensating for it with royal grace." (Mumford, L. 1986)

98   See e.g.: Hammer, Wolfgang (2020, 2021)

21.5.a   Mythomania

Instead of a realistic identity founded on a continuous confrontation with reality, stories are invented to confirm and establish a special position for one's own personality.

The normal leap of faith[99] that people take due to their social orientation makes these mythomaniac creations difficult to recognize as such, at least at first.

21.5.b   Name-Dropping

Part of mythomania is name-dropping, i.e. listing the many supposedly important people with whom the narcissist is in supposedly close contact.

Objectively, however, these people do not have to be of particular importance, nor does a relationship with them actually exist.

And one and the same person can be portrayed as both particularly important and particularly reprehensible – depending on the occasion.

21.5.c   Fundamental Attribution Error

Failure is attributed to circumstances, (random) success to oneself.

Like the landlord who has already driven five bars into the ground, but only blames the circumstances for this.

The manager who has ruined several companies, but takes credit for random, purely statistically necessary improvements.

---

99   See also: Cialdini, Robert (1984)

21.6 Devaluation of the environment

EVERYTHING threatens one's own, unrealistic kingdom. So everything is the enemy, everything must be devalued. Not just to elevate oneself. But also for that purpose.

The king is everything - the people are nothing.

And as a necessary counterpole, one's own ego is glorified, the narcissist feels superior, be it due to self-proclaimed expertise and/or the narcissistic feeling of moral superiority. The climate activists of the "Last Generation"[100] etc. can serve as a current example here.

As self-proclaimed experts who, with no sense of wrongdoing but with the narcissistic feeling of moral superiority, take it upon themselves to coerce and harass other people...

Furthermore, a corresponding reverential attitude is expected from the environment. Here too, vassals are reliable and necessary.

21.7 Denial of reality

The fact that narcissists have to ignore or deny reality should be understandable after the above explanations.

But the fact that this denial of reality, e.g. calling undesirable perspectives "fake news", is even possible to this extent has two prerequisites. Firstly, there are the degrees of freedom within an affluent society that have already been described.

The second is the traditional dogmas that claim that there is ONE truth, that there is a TRUTH.

In recent decades, these dogmas have at least partially dissolved, and with them the truth. Post-factual talk arose.

---

100 This is of course also an example of "antagonistic symbiotic narcissism" (Schmidt, B.; Ganz, A. 2017)

However, if one abandons the idea of truth in favor of the concept of effectiveness ("Wirk-heit" instead of "Wahr-heit"), then one can admit that the creationists' view of a claim to truth is not necessarily inferior to the theory of evolution.

However, in terms of effectiveness, it is.

21.7.a   Digression: effectiveness[101]

The dogma that is probably the most difficult to overcome is that of TRUTH.

It is often overlooked that the path from the Greek origin of the ideas of truth to us was not uninterrupted. Between the loss of Greek philosophy in Western Europe and its return there were several centuries that were shaped purely by Catholicism as a religious monoculture. And this was based on a God who is in possession of pure truth, on representatives of God who also believed themselves to be in possession of this truth.

When Greek philosophy was rediscovered in the Middle Ages, it was as the "handmaiden of theology".

Thus, one can read in Thomas Aquinas: "Whatever proves to be in contradiction with theology in the other sciences must be rejected as false." [quoted from Hirschberger, 1949]

The concept of truth is used in so many different ways that the article on it in Wikipedia is very long. A central point, however, is the concept of truth in logic, which in turn is the basis for the theoretical foundations of science. According to this, a logical statement is true if it is consistent within itself.

But Vaihinger shows that this consistency is in no way necessary to arrive at useful results. Vaihinger distinguishes between "real fictions", which not only contradict reality but are also contradictory within themselves, and "semi-fictions", which only contradict reality. Both types of fiction can lead to useful,

---

101   Auszug von www.b-j-schmidt.net

145

effective results.

Any analytical analysis is at least a semi-fiction (see e.g. G.H. Lewes).

And although there is a broad consensus in both the natural sciences and psychology (see e.g. Watzlawick) that there is no such thing as truth, this term and the ideas associated with it continue to haunt us. Or there is a confusion of terms, as in the title of Paul Watzlawick's book "How real is reality?"

Reality is real, otherwise it would not be reality. But it is simply not true. So the title should actually be "How true is reality?" And just as elephants and bats, as bionomic species, live in different realities, in different physiological meaning and action frameworks, so do psychonomic species. Different scientific schools are to be understood as psychonomic species. With different "frames of meaning" and "frames of practice". This answers the questions raised by TS Kuhn and at the same time explains why, according to Max Planck, the proponents of an old theory that contradicts the new one are not convinced, but die out.

From a psychonomic point of view, the oath formula "... the truth, and nothing but the truth" has become untenable. At most, it would be possible to swear that one is not consciously lying. But the result still usually has little or nothing to do with truth. That is why I am introducing the concept of EFFECTI-VENESS.

Effectiveness is never absolute, but always has a more-less relationship. For example, one theory can have a higher or lower effectiveness than another.

Scientific fictions therefore claim effectiveness, whereas dogmas claim an absolute, sole truth.

The denial of reality consists primarily in not considering alternative approaches to one's own understanding, but completely negating them as "fake news".

There is only one side to the coin.

The denial of reality (""Wirk-lichkeit""), the avoidance of dealing with alternative positions, prevents necessary learning processes and thus personality development... and leads to a profound developmental disorder.

"Einer der bezeichnendsten Züge des neurotischen Verhaltens ist das Unvermögen des Patienten, aus Erfahrungen zu lernen. Er manövriert sich, wie unter einem bösen Fluch, immer wieder in die gleiche Art von verwickelten Situationen hinein und begeht stets die gleichen Irrtümer." (Koestler, A. 1980)[102]

22   Interaction with reality

A disruption of the relationship to reality is both cause and effect.
The disruption of the relationship to reality is the cause due to the previously mentioned paths of pathogenesis via
• traumatization, whether this is
◦ singular or continuous,
◦ objective or subjective
• lack of comprehensibility and thus a lack of feeling of manageability,
• "hedonistic experiencing" (Vasilyuk)
As a result, the narcissistic personality, dissociated from the

---

102 "One of the most characteristic features of neurotic behavior is the patient's inability to learn from experience. He maneuvers himself, as if under an evil curse, into the same kind of complicated situations again and again and always makes the same mistakes." (Koestler, A. 1980)

primary personality, is formed with a rigid SOC (Antonovsky). In the narcissistic personality, the ego is the „Ding" ("Dönig"), who is at the top of the class pyramid.

Without other people on an equal footing, and at the same time as far removed from reality as possible. The connection to reality is made solely through the vassals.

The Ding rules in his own realm, separated from reality, his golden cage, because he has experienced reality as threatening and unmanageable. The "cosmopolitan, curious being" (Konrad Lorenz) becomes a world-weary, anxiety being, dominated by inner compulsions. This affects all areas of interaction with reality.

22.1   Relationship structure

Since the world, including the social world, is perceived as threatening and neither understandable nor manageable (Antonovsky), healthy socio-emotional development is not possible. The narcissist does not develop a mature personality that can enter into an open dialogue with the environment, either in the primary personality (which remains at a childlike level) or in the narcissistic personality. The narcissist thus remains the Ding, isolated from reality, in his own realm of illusion.

22.1.a   Friend or foe

Since there are no people on the same level as the Ding, and by definition there shouldn't be, there are no friends either. Friends would also require a confrontation with one's own mistakes as well as reality. The Ding has no friends, only vassals. Higher and lower vassals, all of whom must be dependent on the Ding, be it emotionally and/or financially.

22.1.b   Allies

Sometimes there are also "allies" in the sense of "Symbiotischer Narzissismus als Gruppenphänomen" (Schmidt, B.;
Ganz, A. 2017). But these allies also only serve as a means, and
are taken advantage of when the opportunity arises. The non-
aggression pact between Hitler and Stalin can serve as an example here. But sometimes quite stable structures of symbiotic
narcissism are formed, which only collapse when an adjust-
ment is necessary due to changes in reality (e.g. due to the corona pandemic or the energy crisis), but is not possible due to,
among other things, rigid SOC (Antonovsky) and "hedonistic
experiencing" (Vasilyuk).

22.1.c   Vasalls

Since reality is perceived as threatening, the narcissist's constant goal is to expand and consolidate his own empire. To do
this, he needs vassals, as this is the only way to contact reality.
The main characteristic of the vassal is his dependence on the
Ding, be it emotional and/or financial. The Ding therefore tries
to draw other people into his own microcosm and make them
his vassals.

This is done primarily through manipulative behavior and manipulative communication[103], such as:

• Only enough is given until you think you have the fish on the
hook.

• The end of the sausage is held in front of your nose.

---

103   In his book "Influence" (1984), Robert Cialdini not only deals with
various forms of manipulation, but also discusses ways to defend
yourself against them. The basic problem that emerges is that manipulation is always based on normal, socially accepted and necessary
behavior and therefore cannot be recognized as such right from the
start.

• You are the greatest daddy in the world, but ... if I don't get the lollipop, you are the dumbest daddy in the world, I don't like you anymore.

Narcissists have it easiest here with (their) children, who are by nature both emotionally and financially dependent. Narcissists do not shy away from using their own children as a means, as vassals[104].

In order to ensure the loyalty of the vassals and their dependence, the other side of the "rabble-rousing-continuum" comes into play. The vassals are bullied and harassed to prove their loyalty to Dönig. This can be as simple as having to salute the "Gessler hat" or even a "brainfuck".

For example, narcissists like to "give" you money without clearly defining the conditions. This means that these "debts" can be used to humiliate you at any time.

22.2   Communication and Interaction[105]

A central and important problem with narcissists is the narcissism trap. Narcissists can hardly change their behavior because they perceive changes as dangerous and threatening. This also means that, on the one hand, personality development is almost impossible. On the other hand, reassessing a critical situation and adapting to a changing reality is impossible.

The ability to forgive insults, e.g. through criticism, is also necessary for personality development. But this is largely lacking in narcissists.

---

104 See e.g. Schmidt, B. (2020c)

105 The following section was taken largely unchanged from (Schmidt, B.; Ganz, A. 2017).

22.2.a   Communication

The need to avoid contact with reality as a measure of self-worth and to avoid anxiety-inducing changes, while at the same time satisfying the need for effectiveness, naturally also has a (negative) effect on the communication structure of narcissists. Communication is a form of interaction with reality (perceived as threatening).

22.2.b   No discussion on the substantive level

If one distinguishes between factual and relational levels in communication, it is clear that narcissists are hardly capable of discourse on the factual level, at least in relevant aspects. This is because the debate on the factual level involves critical contact with reality as a measure of one's own actions. Therefore, an attack or a shift to the relational level usually occurs.

It is not the (controversial) issue or theory that is criticized, but the person(s) who represent it. Not only is a statement or criticism not evaluated independently of the speaker, but on the contrary, only the opponent as a person is usually discredited and attacked[106].

The result is a personalization instead of differentiation of criticism and problems - and this is sometimes tangible, as for example at Donald Trump's first election rallies, where critics were also knocked down and thrown out of the hall.

22.2.c   Narcissistic-destructive communication

Instead of a constructive (self-)critical dialogue, one finds a pronounced narcissistic-destructive communication. The idea of thesis, antithesis and synthesis is a distant memory for narcissists. Out of anxiety of reality and change, narcissists use

---

106 See e.g. Schmidt, B. (2017)

both attacks against the person of the "opponent" and rhetorical subtleties as a defense.

Such "discussions" can and should lead to nothing other than the confirmation of the narcissistic self-image. And this is usually at the expense of the "discussion" partner, who is devalued as a person.

22.2.d   No meta-level

An interesting phenomenon in narcissists is the extensive inability to analyse - especially their own behaviour - on a meta-level. Critically examining one's own actions from a more objective, higher-level perspective and in interaction with the environment is, understandably, almost impossible. Narcissists are thus denied access to the insight that one cannot refute the accusation of narcissistic (destructive) behaviour by continuing the very behaviour that is being criticized. Instead, the critic is usually attacked as a person, as already mentioned. The extensive lack of reflection on a meta-level is another important building block for the "narcissism trap".

22.3   Communication triangle

The communication structure of narcissists described above can be clearly illustrated by a modification of the four-sided model of communication by Schulz von Thun (1981).
In the original version, there are the levels of **relationship** and **matter**, as well as the sides of **self-disclosure** and **appeal**.

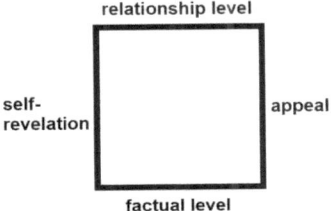

In the communication of narcissists, the factual level is necessarily lost due to the denial of reality already explained.

At the same time, there is a difference between the compulsive self-presentation on the one hand and the self-revelation generated by it on the other.

Self-revelation is ignored in narcissistic communication just as much as the factual level. This is how we get the emperor who wants to present himself in his new clothes in the spirit of self-presentation, but because of the self-revelation he stands naked before his people.

The communication rectangle becomes a triangle in which there is only the relationship level and the appeal, because the factual level and self-revelation are ignored.

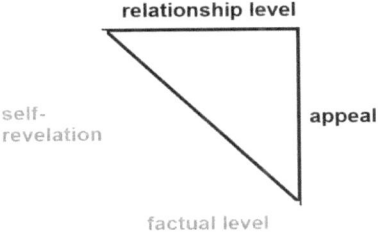

Attempts to discuss the matter with narcissists are always met with an effort to immediately move the discussion to the relationship level, accompanied by appeals to the other person[107].

---

107 See also: Schmidt, Bernhard J. (2021): Praktische Psychologie für den Sicherheitsdienst.

Whoever justifies himself ...

If someone defends themselves, does he automatically accuse himself?
No, a defense is not necessarily the same as self-accusation. Self-accusation only arises from the lack of awareness of the factual level and, above all, self-revelation.
The right to refuse to testify is useful in this respect, even if narcissists rarely make use of it. The pressure to present oneself is too great.

22.3.a   Triangle of Criticism

If we apply the four-sided model of communication to criticism, we have the levels of **form** and **content**, as well as the sides of **criticism** and **self-disclosure**. The latter is often overlooked by critics.

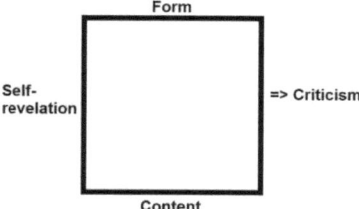

Even with criticism as a special form of communication, narcissists necessarily lose the level of reality, in this case the content. And as with general communication, self-revelation is not perceived in criticism either. Here, too, the rectangle becomes a triangle.

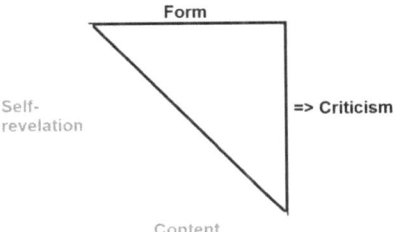

Narcissistic criticism is limited to the form alone as a basis, because this avoids dealing with the content and thus with reality. Examples of this can be found in the negative reviews of my books, in which only (!) the form is criticized (completely rightly, since I care less about the form than the content) so that the content does not have to be dealt with at all.

Reality is simply ignored, as in a review in which the reviewer complains that the book is too short and contains too few scientific citations.

The book, however, was published in the "Klartext kompakt" series with the title "Das Asperger Syndrom – für Schulbegleiter".

Here, as is usual with narcissists, the author's own wishes have overshadowed the perception of reality.

Narcissistic criticism can be recognized by the fact that it is never balanced, but always only concerns the form and in no way the content.

22.3.b   The bullying-manipulating continuum

The central problem for narcissists is to act, at least peripherally, in a reality that must be ignored at the same time. As already described, it is therefore important to draw other people into one's own illusory world or perception bubble as vassals.

155

On the other hand, there is the need to elevate one's own ego and devalue everyone else in order to feel safe as a Ding („Dönig") in one's own realm. In combination with the need for effectiveness[108] , this creates a continuum between

manipulating, instrumentalizing, ignoring

<=======>

bullying, harassment

The areas cannot be clearly separated, but can overlap or change in relatively short rhythms.

Manipulating, instrumentalizing, ignoring

The area of manipulation, instrumentalization and ignoring primarily serves to integrate other people into one's own false world without having to deal with reality.
As social beings who actively negotiate meaning socially (Wenger), people give their fellow human beings a certain amount of trust[109]. This is mercilessly exploited by narcissists. Emotional and financial traps are set up to convey interest and acceptance of the other person. The other person is only to be used as a means and never as an end in itself. The aim is always, as already described, to make the other person financially and/or emotionally dependent.
The other person is manipulated, instrumentalized as a means, and their personality, especially in the area of existing skills, is ignored.

---

108 See also: Schmidt, Bernhard J.; Ganz, Andreas (2017): Symbiotischer Narzissmus als Gruppenphänomen.
109 See also: Cialdini, Robert (1984)

Bullying, harassment

If the Ding is fairly sure of a vassal, the manipulative behavior turns into the opposite, into insulting, bullying and harassment. Many employees have experienced this change first hand, especially in areas where dependency is particularly high. This is especially true in the low-wage sector, where employees' degrees of freedom are usually very low due to a lack of qualifications.

23   Aftereffects

As a result of what has been described so far, further aspects of the symptom complex described at the beginning arise - and this is inevitable! The aspects that justify both the designation "asshole" and "illness" come to light.

23.1   Entitlement mentality

"I am the Dönig!" is the credo of narcissists. Because you want it, it has to be that way. Even if your own expectations are in no way compatible with reality. The catering and hotel industry offer a wide range of experiences, for example through guests who expect services that they do not even come close to paying for (or want to pay for), who want to be recognized and treated as special guests...
The Dönig also does not accept "impossible"; his will is a command.

23.2   Lack of empathy / pseudo-empathy

Without successful interaction with the environment, without the development of comprehensibility and manageability, the socio-emotional development of narcissists fails, as already shown. And thus also the development of empathy, which also requires an engagement with reality and does not only view the animate and inanimate environment as a means. On the one hand, this leads to a complete lack of any empathy, a lack of perception of the environment as an end in itself. Realized, for example, in the operators of factory farming, merciless exploitation and pollution of nature, always under the dictate of profit maximization, the satisfaction of one's own greed.

On the other hand, structures with pronounced pseudo-empathy form as "antagonistic symbiotic narcissism" (Schmidt, B; Ganz, A. 2017), such as in animal welfare (see Schmidt, B. 2022).

23.3   Destruction and lack of awareness of wrong-doing

The Dönig is the ruler in his own kingdom, without orientation towards reality, with the need for effectiveness, in combination with ignoring the factual level, based on "rigid SOC" (Antonovsky) and "hedonistic experiencing" (Vasilyuk).

This combination inevitably leads, sooner or later, to (auto)destructive behavior.

Narcissists destroy children, families, companies... animate and inanimate nature... and ultimately themselves.

The Pope's dogma of infallibility can also be found in narcissists. It is based on the lack of ability to be self-critical because it requires a confrontation with reality. The Dönig is the ruler in his own apparent kingdom, which is why he also lacks any sense of wrongdoing. His kingdom - his rules.

The Dönig cannot, in principle, do wrong.

The environment in all its forms is always only a means, never an end in itself.

23.4 Dogmatism, ideology, intolerance, missionary work

The elements already discussed that have shaped the narcissism of Western culture over the last 1,700 years can also be found in the narcissistic individual.

It is dogmatism that limits thinking to a small part of reality and excludes the rest. This is what makes one's own kingdom possible.

At the same time, there is always an "exclusive promise of salvation", an ideology, both for the Dönig himself and for his vassals. Esotericism is of great use here.

Intolerance towards other positions, life plans, etc. is just as necessary for the defense and stabilization of one's own false world as proselytizing.

The latter also serves as a justification for bullying and harassment, as well as for the exploitation of other people.

Children who stick to the streets because of climate change can serve as an example of proselytizing or bullying.

23.5 Lack of action competence and problem-solving skills

Due to the disturbed relationship to reality, the anxiety of it, the actions required to develop action competence and problem-solving skills are not possible in reality. The narcissistic personality is characterized by "hedonistic exeriencing".

The lack of action and problem-solving skills and the escape into the narcissistic personality as a compensation are the components that attach "illness" to the term "asshole".

23.6   Illness

The inability to act in reality, to satisfy the desire for effectiveness, to have fulfilling relationships instead of vassal status,
etc. inevitably lead to illness. This manifests itself primarily
through two symptoms - recurrent depression and persistent addiction problems.

23.6.a   Recurrent depression

Let us approach the question of the causes of recurring depression in narcissists this time through the theologian and "General Teacher of Christianity", Thomas Aquinas (1225-1274).

"The search for truth always throws the active mind back on
itself. "Truth, as Thomas explained in De veritate I,9, is only
possible through self-reflection, the return of thought to itself."
Thus Thomas says in [STh] 93,4: "The highest imitation of
God, however, consists for the spiritual nature in the imitation
of his self-knowledge and self-love." (Schmidt, B. 2015)

But how do self-knowledge and self-love fit together? Recognizing your own shortcomings and mistakes with self-love?
There is neither the space nor the need to explain this here.
This basic conflict should help us understand the problem of
depression in narcissists.
Because self-love WITHOUT self-knowledge is narcissism.
And the other side of the coin, self-knowledge WITHOUT self-
love, is a form of depression.
When the one-sided self-aggrandizement, megalomania, which
is not confirmed by any external experience in practical and so-
cial life, in reality, collapses, then depression is the result.
But in order to even enable a solid self-perception anchored in

reality, a self-critical attitude would be necessary. But this is missing and must be missing due to the repression of reality. The king is never wrong and the pope is infallible.

The narcissistic self-concept is always, as already described, a vulnerable self-concept. Maintaining one's own false world, the kingdom of evil, requires a lot of energy and never allows the narcissist to rest. The narcissist is almost always on the defensive.[110] Exhaustion can also be the cause of depression.

23.6.b   Persistent addiction problem

Not all alcoholics are narcissists, but many narcissists are alcoholics or have other addictions.

Maintaining the narcissistic illusion requires a lot of energy, so the easy way to block out reality through addictive behavior is obvious. Especially since the narcissistic personality as a whole is dominated by compulsions.

> "Why do you drink? To forget.
> What do you want to forget? That I drink."

24   Countermeasures

Narcissism is in no way "fascinating", as quoted at the beginning. Narcissists can be described as parasitic due to their manipulative behavior, their efforts to bring others into economic and/or emotional dependency and thus exploit them as vassals.

This is also how we should address the question of how we can free ourselves from the clutches of narcissists if we have fallen into their clutches. How we can get rid of the parasite again.

---

110 It is the rare situations that the narcissist perceives as safe in which the primary personality emerges.

24.1   Separation

If emotionally and financially possible, then immediately separating from the narcissist is the safest and best way.
However, this option rarely occurs because, as shown, narcissists do everything in their power to make their victims emotionally and/or financially dependent and keep them there.
Sometimes fate helps, for example in the form of an inheritance, to at least free oneself from financial dependence. Sometimes one is faced with the question of whether one would rather bite off one's own paw like the fox in the trap in order to escape.

24.2   Avoid criticism

Narcissists not only feel massively threatened by criticism, but also see it as an insult to the majesty of the person.
The ability to take criticism requires confronting reality as well as one's own weaknesses. But narcissists cannot do either.
The narcissist being criticized is also extremely resentful and vengeful. Criticizing the narcissist therefore achieves nothing – except further trouble.

24.3   Stay objective

As already shown, narcissists will always try to draw a critic to the relationship level.
For example, through praise or insults (see manipulation-insulting continuum).
They are not capable of constructive solutions, because these would require a confrontation with reality.
Therefore: always remain objective and constructive!
Against all attacks on the relationship level.
Over and over again.

24.4   Counter-manipulation

As great masters of manipulation as narcissists usually are,
they are equally susceptible to manipulation themselves.
While manipulability is usually based on the exploitation of social behavior[111], the manipulability of narcissists has other
roots.
Manipulability arises from the constant devaluation of the environment and a lack of awareness of differences in competence,
a lack of self-criticism and the inability to analyze problems on
a meta-level.
Narcissists therefore believe everything that fits into their exaggerated self-image and their own goals (e.g. making the other
person dependent).
Counter-manipulation thus offers a way to free oneself from
dependence on narcissists[112].

24.5   Therapy

Narcissism is generally considered impossible to treat, as is the
case with rabies.
The reasons for the resistance of narcissism to treatment can
only be understood from the perspective presented here.
The primary ego remains, but at a childlike level. There is no
development into a mature personality, which is why a permanent return to the primary personality (in contrast to a return
that may occur sporadically) is not possible.
The development of narcissistic personalities, on the other
hand, has proven successful, at least in the short term.
As the narcissistic personality is not capable of adapting to cri-

---

111   See e.g.: Cialdini, Robert (1984)

112   See also: Schmidt, B. (2018b)

tical situations and of reassessing or changing behavior, new narcissistic personalities form when previous compensation is no longer possible. Just as supposedly normal, well-integrated people become "Querdenker" due to a crisis, for example, and join forces in the form of "symbiotic narcissism" (Schmidt, B.; Ganz, A. 2017).

PROGNOSIS

Once generalized symptoms have developed, the prognosis is unfavorable, both in the case of narcissism and rabies.

In the case of individual narcissism, as well as in the case of societal narcissism. In the case of the latter, not because Western society is narcissistic, but because it offers the degrees of freedom to develop narcissistic personality disorders and structures.

It is difficult to determine how large the proportion of narcissists in society really is.

But even a small proportion is enough to lead an affluent society to self-destructive ruin.

And this is due to the characteristics described, which are always superior to a reality-based, weighing-up attitude:

• Dogmatism
• Ideology
• Intolerance
• Missionization

These are additionally stabilized by antagonistic symbiotic narcissism structures (Schmidt, B.; Ganz, A. 2017), which lead to a fruitless polarization of any discussion.

Reason, based on measure and balance, is lost - it is now only an either-or situation. Animal abusers or animal rights activists, climate saviors or climate sinners, vegans or animal and climate killers...

Society is increasingly dominated by people who deny reality, but are equipped with a narcissistic feeling of moral superiority.

But the world will not end, as predicted by "Extinction Rebellion" and "Last Generation", for example; no, it will change, as it has always done since its existence.

Nature will not disappear as a result of human activity either. It will change, as it has always done. Even after greater catastrophes than those represented by the supposed "homo sapiens". And humanity will not end either, having survived greater catastrophes.

The strange (WEIRD) Western culture will end as a psychonomic species. Just like the culture of the Romans, on whose territory the Italians now live.

The prophecies with which we are constantly confronted stem primarily from one cause:

the narcissistic overvaluation of one's own existence.

It is not humans who are, as Arthur Köstler believes, a stray of evolution, but rather Western culture. They are the "predatory apes in cultural disguise", as Theodor Lessing calls us.

But humans are and remain mayflies (Rupert Riedel) who have to cope with their position of nothingness in the face of the universe (Blaise Pascal).

If we want to preserve reason,
then we must overcome belief in it.

BIBLIOGRAPHY

Adler, Alfred (1912): Über den nervösen Charakter

Antonovsky, Aaron (Hg.) (1997): Salutogenese. Zur Entmystifizierung der Gesundheit. Tübingen: Dgvt-Verl. (Forum für Verhaltenstherapie und psychosoziale Praxis, 36).

Bakker, P. (1987): Autonomous languages of twins. In: *Acta geneticae medicae et gemellologiae* 36 (2), S. 233–238.
DOI: 10.1017/S0001566000004463.

Bassin, F. V. (1978): Unbewusstes und Verhalten

Benedict, Ruth (1934): Anthropology and the Abnormal. In: *The Journal of General Psychology* 10 (1), S. 59–82.
DOI: 10.1080/00221309.1934.9917714.

Bergmeier, Rolf (2018): Machtkampf. Die Geburt der Staatskirche : vom Sieg des Katholizismus und den Folgen für Europa. Erste Auflage 2018. Aschaffenburg: Alibri Verlag.

Blum, Deborah (2010): Die Entdeckung der Mutterliebe. Die legendären Affenexperimente des Harry Harlow. Weinheim: Beltz. Online verfügbar unter http://www.content-select.com/index.php?id=bib_view&ean=978-3-407-22489-7.

Bowlby, John (1980): Attachment and loss. Vol II: separation; anxiety and anger. Reprint with corrections. London

Broad, William; Wade, Nicholas (1982): Betrayers of the truth. New York, NY: Simon and Schuster.

Bühler, Karl (1927: Die Krise der Psychologie

Cialdini, Robert B. (1984): Influence. The new psychology of modern persuasion

Dörner, Klaus; Plog, Ursula (1984): Irren ist menschlich oder Lehrbuch der Psychiatrie/Psychotherapie. 8. Aufl. Rehburg-Loccum

Edelman, Gerald (2005): Wider than the sky. The phenomenal gift of consciousness.

Eibl-Eibesfeldt, Irenäus (2004): Die Biologie des menschlichen Verhaltens. Grundriß der Humanethologie. 5. Aufl.

Festinger, Leon; Riecken, Henry W.; Schachter, Stanley (2012): When prophecy fails. A social and psychological study of a modern group that predicted the destruction of the world.

Hassin; Uleman; Bargh (2005): The New Unconscious

Koestler, Arthur (1965): Diesseits von Gut und Böse. Bern: Scherz.

Koestler, Arthur (1980): Die Armut der Psychologie. Der Mensch als Opfer des Versuchs, irrationalem Verhalten mit rationalen Methoden beizukommen. 1. Aufl. Bern: Scherz.

Kropotkin, Pëtr Alekseevič (1902): Mutual Aid. A factor of evolution. London: Heinemann.

Lasch, Christopher (1980): Das Zeitalter des Narzißmus. München: Steinhausen.

Lave, Jean; Wenger, Etienne (1991): Situated Learning. Legitimate Peripheral Participation

Lessing, Theodor (1930): Der jüdische Selbsthaß. Berlin: Jüdischer Verl.

Lessing, Theodor (1929/2021): Europa und Asien. Untergang der Erde am Geist. 1. Auflage. Hg. v. BERNHARD J. SCHMIDT. Norderstedt: Books on Demand (REdition Schmidt, 20).

Levy, David M. (1943): Maternal Overprotection

Lewes, George Henry (1874): Problems of Life and Mind

Lowen, Alexander (1992): Narzissmus. Die Verleugnung des wahren Selbst. 1. Aufl. München: Goldmann (Goldmann, 12314).

Morf, Carolyn C.; Rhodewalt, Frederick (2001): Unraveling the Paradoxes of Narcissism: A Dynamic Self-Regulatory Processing Model. In: *Psychological Inquiry* 12 (4), S. 177–196. DOI: 10.1207/S15327965PLI1204_1.

Morgan, Conwy Lloyd (1894): An introduction to comparative psychology. London (The Contemporary science series). Online verfügbar unter http://searcn.ebscohost.com/direct.asp?db=pzh&jid=%22200622788%22&scope=site.

Mumford, Lewis (1986): Mythos der Maschine. Kultur, Technik u. Macht ; [die umfassende Darstellung der Entdeckung und Entwicklung der Technik. Ungekürzte Ausg., 29. - 31. Tsd. Frankfurt am Main

Pavlov, I. P.: Psychopathology and Psychiatry. Selected Works

Pieper, Josef (1991): Das Viergespann. Klugheit, Gerechtigkeit, Tapferkeit, Mass. 6. Aufl., 39. - 41. Tsd. München: Kösel.

Postman, Neil (1988): Wir amüsieren uns zu Tode. 7. Aufl.

Richter, Horst Eberhard (1982): Der Gotteskomplex. Die Geburt und die Krise des Glaubens an die Allmacht des Menschen. 81. - 85. Tsd.

Romanes, G. John (1885/2021): Die geistige Entwicklung im Tierreich. Nebst einer nachgelassenen Arbeit: "Über den Instinkt" von Charles Darwin. 1. Auflage. Hg. v. BERNHARD J. SCHMIDT. Norderstedt: Books on Demand (REdition Schmidt, 2).

Scherrer, Lucien (2021): Politisches Mobbing an der Universität: der Fall Klaus Kinzler. In: *Neue Zürcher Zeitung*, 14.09.2021. Online verfügbar unter https://www.nzz.ch/feuilleton/diskussion-beendet-ld.1644831, zuletzt geprüft am 22.12.2021.

Schmidt, Bernhard Johannes (2015): Vernunft und Freiheit. Bei Thomas von Aquin. Norderstedt: Books on Demand.

Schmidt, Bernhard J. (2017): Autismus und der Kühlschrankmutter Mythos. Eine Rehabilitierung Bruno Bettelheims. Norderstedt: Books on Demand (Beiträge zur Wissenschaftspsychologie, 3).

Schmidt, Bernhard J. (2018a): BauSÄTZE: Frames - als Be-Deu-tungs-Rahmen. Beiträge zur Wissens(chafts)-Psychologie. 1. Auflage. Norderstedt: Books on Demand (BauSÄTZE, 2).

Schmidt, Bernhard J. (2018b): Autist und Suizid: Ringen mit der Option Tod. Norderstedt: Books on Demand

Schmidt, Bernhard J. (2020a): DOGmatismus. Neue Perspektiven auf Mensch, Hund und Kultur. 1. Auflage. Norderstedt: BoD – Books on Demand.

Schmidt, Bernhard J. (2020b): Entwurf einer wissenschaftlichen Psychologie. 1. Auflage. Norderstedt: BoD - Books on Demand.

Schmidt, Bernhard J. (2020c): Das Münchhausen Stellvertreter Syndrom als Gruppenphänomen. 1. Auflage. Norderstedt: BoD - Books on Demand

Schmidt, Bernhard J. (2021): Praktische Psychologie für den Sicherheitsdienst. 1. Auflage. Norderstedt: BoD - Books on Demand.

Schmidt, Bernhard J. (2022): Zur Psychopathologie institutionalisierter Misshandlungen. 1. Auflage. Norderstedt: BoD - Books on Demand.

Schmidt, Bernhard J.; Ganz, Andreas (2016): Klartext kompakt. Das Asperger Syndrom – nicht nur für Psychotherapeuten. Norderstedt: Books on Demand

Schmidt, Bernhard J.; Ganz, Andreas (2017): Symbiotischer Narzissmus als Gruppenphänomen. Norderstedt: Books on Demand

Schulz von Thun, Friedemann (1981): Miteinander reden 1

Skinner, B. F. (1948): Superstition in the pigeon

Smedslund, J. (2009): The Mismatch between Current Research Methods and the Nature of Psychological Phenomena

Thurnwald, Richard (1932): Economics in primitve communities

Turner, John C. (2005): Explaining the nature of power: A three-process theory

Tyler, Imogen (2007): From `The Me Decade' to `The Me Millennium'. In: *International Journal of Cultural Studies* 10 (3), S. 343–363. DOI: 10.1177/1367877907080148.

Vaihinger, Hans (1923): Die Philosophie des „als ob"

Vasilyuk, Fedor Efimovich (1988): The psychology of experiencing. An analysis of how critical situations are dealt with. Moscow: Progress Publishers.

Vygotskij, Lev Semenovič (2017): Denken und Sprechen. Psychologische Untersuchungen. Unter Mitarbeit von Alexandre Metraux. 3., neu ausgestattete Auflage. Weinheim, Basel: Beltz.

Vygotskij, Lev Semenovič; Cole, Michael (1981): Mind in society. The development of higher psychological processes. [Nachdr.]. Cambridge, Mass.: Harvard Univ. Press.

Vygotskij, Lev Semenovič; Glick, Joseph (1997): The history of the development of higher mental functions. New York: Plenum Press (The collected works of L. S. Vygotsky, 4).

Vygotskij, Lev Semenovič; Luria, Aleksandr Romanovich; Golod, Victor I.; Knox, Jane Elizabeth (Hg.) (1993): Studies on the history of behavior. Ape, primitive, and child. Hillsdale, NJ: Erlbaum.

Wagoner; Christensen; Demuth (2021): Culture as Process

Wenger, Etienne (1998/2016): Communities of Practice

Wertsch, James V. (1985): Vygotsky and the Social Formation of Mind. Cambridge: Harvard University Press.

Wolfe, Tom (1976): The me decade and the third great awakening. In: *New York Magazine*. Online verfügbar unter http://theological-geography.net/wp-content/uploads/2018/09/tom-wolfe.pdf.

Wundt, Wilhelm (1913): Elemente der Völkerpsychologie

Zittoun, Tania; Gillespie, Alex & Cornish, Flora (2009): Fragmentation or differentiation: Questioning the crisis in psychology

Narcissism